THE **IMPOSSIBLE** MADE **POSSIBLE**

A PARAPLEGIC'S INCREDIBLE ODYSSEY ACROSS AMERICA

ROB BRYANT

Jo Ji Morow

BROADMAN PRESS
NASHVILLE, TENNESSEE

©Copyright 1991 ● Broadman Press

All rights reserved

4253-50

ISBN: 0-8054-5350-4

Dewey Decimal Classification: B

Subject Heading: BRYANT, ROB // HANDICAPPED - BIOGRAPHY

Library of Congress Card Catalog Number: 91-741

Printed in the United States of America

Library of Congress Cataloging-in-Publication Data

Bryant, Rob, 1955-
   The impossible made possible / Rob Bryant.
     p. cm.
   Sequel to: Lord, lift me up.
   ISBN 0-8054-5350-4
    1. Bryant, Rob, 1955-   . 2. Christian biography—United States.
   3. Paraplegics—United States—Biography. 4. Christian life—1960—
   I. Title.
   BR1725.B72A3   1991
209'.2—dc20   91-741
[B]   CIP

To Steve and Kristi,
my parents,
my friends Jeff and Don,
other team members and friends,
and to Wanice, Jason, and Jonathan
who were always there when I needed them

Contents

1

What Next, Lord?—

In Search of God's Will

Pull, Rob! Pull! I yelled at myself as I laboriously yanked on the handles of my RowCycle, a three-wheeled rowing machine. Each pull on the handles required approximately 100 pounds of pressure. I would have to pull on the handles at least 10,000 more times merely to row over this one hill!

As a matter of fact, I was warned by a number of fellow athletes that my mission of rowing clear across America would be "mission impossible." After rowing half the day, I had covered only twenty miles. I had a staggering 3,000 miles ahead of me. I was wondering how I was ever going to make it. I was in the Mojave Desert on the side of a mountain, almost out of water, and completely exhausted. This early in my odyssey, I was moving in and out of reality as I incessantly rowed on those handles and looked at the barrenness surrounding me.

The desert disappeared in every direction. The sun beat down on my brother Steve and me as the dryness and heat sapped the life from our bodies. Steve, riding a bike beside me, was carrying seventy pounds of tools and extra water. Although riding a bike was much easier than rowing, he nevertheless was sweating at the task. *Have I made a mistake in attempting this* Guinness World Record *of rowing?* I wondered.

Honk. Honk. A truck zoomed by, the driver waving at us enthusiastically. Maybe this trucker had heard about what I was attempting to do. Steve and I were boosted by the trucker's encouragement and continued up the steep grade.

Pull, Rob! Pull! I prodded myself again. My eyes traveled down the row arms to the body of the RowCycle's sleek-looking frame, then to the brace I was wearing on my right leg. In an effort to escape the pain in my arms, shoulders, back, chest, and stomach, my mind traveled to the past.

Eight years ago I had fallen fifty-five feet from an oil derrick, snapping my spine like a twig. Despite the fact that I could not feel or move from the waist down, I set a goal to walk again. Even with second-degree burns from the knees down, pressure sores, two painful back surgeries, six months in a hospital, and endless challenges, I was able to walk twenty-four miles from Fort Worth to Dallas on braces and crutches, called "The Miracle Walk"—a world record for a paraplegic.

I had written *Lord, Lift Me Up . . .* about those devastating experiences. The words, paragraphs, and chapters seemed to have flowed from me. But, as I prayed, I felt God was not finished with me yet. It seemed that all of the sermons I listened to and the Scriptures I had read, spoke to me concerning my dilemma with the book. These sermons and accounts from God's Word told about men and women who accomplished a monumental task only to find out that the first task was merely a test of faith for a much larger task. For example, God helped David, while he tended his sheep, to slay a lion before the biggest test of faith—facing Goliath. I began to realize that "The Miracle Walk" was a just a test of faith for the next step of faith. I wasn't sure what that step would be, but I assured the Lord I was ready.

One day I read an article about a man who had run across the entire country. Soon afterward I heard about a fellow who pushed his wheelchair across America. I was amazed at the strength and stamina those feats must have required. Inspired by those two, I began pushing my wheelchair a few miles at a time. On one of those occasions I was joined by Randy Ross, the youth minister at our church. I mentioned the articles to him.

"Randy, can you believe that anyone could run or push a wheelchair across the entire country? I get tired just pushing this chair a few miles. I could never do anything like that, could I?"

"I don't know about that," Randy smiled. "I believe you can do anything that God calls you to do. The walk you made to Dallas proved that to me. Maybe the reason this has had such an impact on you is that God is going to call you to do something similar as a testimony of His power."

We were quiet for a long time. His words rang in my ears. His comment seemed ridiculous. I could never do anything like that.

"But that was the point," came a small Voice in my heart.

"You can't, but God can through you. After all, you were supposed to go to prison, but you didn't. You were never supposed to walk again, but you did."

No, this was too much to believe this time. I put it out of my mind and tried to finish the three-mile trip I was on at that moment. But try as I might I could not put it out of my mind.

When I returned home, just for fun, I looked at a United States map.

Since I'm being totally ludicrous anyway, why not put together a route that I would take across the country? I thought.

Let's see. I would start in Los Angeles. I would of course have to pass through my hometown of Fort Worth on the way. A good finishing point would be Washington D.C. Adding up the mileage, it was almost 3,300 miles. I put the map down. What was I trying to do? I was over thirty years old. I was twenty-five pounds overweight and had not done any serious training since "The "Miracle Walk" now over three years ago. This was too much to dare to believe, but I could not shake the feeling that this was the next step of faith. For a few weeks, I prayed that if this was not of God that the impression would go away. But it didn't. It mushroomed. I became obsessed with the idea, and excitement began to replace my fears and doubts.

I began to consider the trip as a soon-to-be reality and examined it logically, not only from blind faith (from God's standpoint, faith is never blind). I felt that I must examine all of the problems I would encounter, do as much about them as I humanly could, and then let God make up the difference. But I did not have a peace that the time was right to go ahead with any concrete plans.

In October of 1987, I went to work at DynCorp as a technical writer and within a year was managing a small department. My new supervisors, Dale Klugman, Phil Britt, Dan Duboise, and Chuck Lievrouw would help me in ways I could not have imagined. My new job should have been enough to satisfy me, but I was not entirely happy with my life. There was a nagging feeling that I was supposed to be planning for the cross-country row. But I still did not know how or when—especially how. God was about to answer both questions.

One evening, my wife Wanice and I were sitting around the kitchen table after dinner. "By the way, Rob, I saw an interesting ad in something that came in today's mail. Look at this," she said, handing me the magazine.

There on the back of a magazine for the disabled was an ad for the weirdest contraption. It was called a RowCycle. Basically, it was a rowing machine on wheels. It was propelled by two handles that looked and acted like oars. The handles were connected to a chain that turned a sprocket on the back wheels. Suddenly I realized that I was looking at the apparatus that God was going to use to propel me across the country. It was as if the picture came alive and I could see myself in the RowCycle crossing the finish line in Washington. If I had known how hard rowing was and that the existing Guinness World Record for land rowing was only 750 miles, I probably would not have been obedient to God. I ordered a RowCycle immediately. Two weeks later, I was riding on the RowCycle. At first, it required a great deal of effort to propel the device. As a matter of fact, the first time I used it, I went only three miles before I became totally exhausted. After six weeks of training, though, I was able to travel over twenty miles over an eight-hour period. Within another month, I was going over thirty-five miles in eight hours. It was painful, yet a tremendous amount of fun. I had forgotten how much I missed riding a bike since my accident, so now I could use my upper body in lieu of my legs.

My dream to cross the country was rekindled, and I began training in earnest. At first Wanice was very skeptical. Soon, though, she became supportive. For me to be successful, Wanice was prepared to make huge sacrifices. My goals were giant and numerous. The first three goals were to publish a book to carry with me across the country, find at least two people to come with me, and secure sponsorship to pay for the traveling expenses.

Now that I had the RowCycle, I sent my manuscript off to six publishers telling them of my plans to cross the country, speaking to churches and selling the book en route. A Broadman editor tried to build support for the manuscript and finally sent it back with regrets. Three days later he called and said, "Rob, I hope you haven't sent it anywhere else. Deep down inside I feel the Holy Spirit wants me to make another stab at it."

That's the rest of the story. Soon after, another prayer was about to be answered. My younger brother Steve and his new wife Kristi were helping me train for the trip by accompanying me on Saturday rowing trips. They were unusually quiet on a particular day, and I could feel that something was out of the ordinary.

"Rob, I want to ask you something," he said in a serious tone. "I had a dream a few nights ago about coming on the 'Row Across America' with you." Of course, I thought he was kidding, so I began laughing and changed the subject.

"No, I'm serious. Kristi and I have talked about it a lot and we feel that God has called us to go with you."

"Steve, think about it for a minute. We'll be gone for over four months. What about your job? Besides, you and Kristi have just been married. How do I know this is what you really want, that you are not just doing this out of some loyalty to your brother? In addition, Kristi loves you so much that she may just be saying she wants to go along out of obedience to her new husband's wishes."

"No," Steve came back, "You don't understand. Kristi is the one who brought it up in the first place. I agree with her. I feel that it's God's will for us to go with you."

I couldn't believe it. Was this true? Had God answered another prayer that quickly? Steve and Kristi were perfect for the trip. Steve was in terrific shape and could ride his bike along with me. Kristi worked for Teen Challenge and was an expert at public relations and raising funds. She would be perfect to stay ahead of us and coordinate the speaking engagements, dealing with the media, and handling other necessities.

"Steve, I want you to think and pray about it for another month. If you still feel this strongly about it, we'll do it together." I waited on pins and needles for their answer. In the meantime, Wanice and I also prayed about it. After one month, they reaffirmed their desire to go along, and I accepted. It was done.

About that time, I had a business trip to the West Coast just before vacationing on the East Coast. The timing was incredible. That would enable me to see where I would start and where I would finish, all within the following two weeks.

While I was in Los Angeles, I saw my friends, the Petersons and Wilsons, and revealed my plans. Jeff Wilson and Bob Peterson had assisted assisted me with "The Miracle Walk" and now helped me plot out the route using various atlases.

After concluding my business on the West Coast, I flew back home to Fort Worth and left for vacation. Wanice, the kids, and I drove clear to Washington, D. C., along the route for my future cross-country trek. But this route was terrible. For one thing, it followed the Appalachian mountains for over 500 miles. Not only that, but there were no shoulders on the roads I had selected. So I replanned the trip from Nashville east to Washington on a new route that would carry me north almost to Columbus, Ohio, and then straight east to Washington. While in Washington, Wanice and I drove past the Capitol building, and both of us were struck with the reality that in less than a year and a half from that day, I would cross a finish line right where we stood. It was a staggering thought. I had a tremendous amount of planning, praying, and training to do. The rest of the week passed quickly. We were back in Fort Worth.

One week after returning home, Wanice, Kristi, Steve, and I started meeting on Mondays for planning and prayer sessions for our trip now less than one year away.

At our first prayer meeting we shared our goals and aspirations. We made a list of the prayer requests:

1. I loved my job. I prayed that my bosses would understand my desire to row across America and that I would have a job when I returned.

2. We still needed sponsorship to pay for the heavy expenses we would incur on our trip.

3. We prayed that God would help us with any improvements to the RowCycle since it might be prone to break down easily.

4. We prayed for God to bless us all with strength, perseverance, and health to sustain us through the trials of our training and goals.

5. We also prayed that Steve's boss would approve a four-month leave of absence with pay and/or benefits, that he would have a job when he returned, and that Kristi would find work.

If we had only known the power of that first prayer meeting, we would have started praying much earlier in the developmental stages of our trip. As a matter of fact, Steve realized as we noticed the date, that the trip was exactly one year away.

I wanted to raise money for a non-profit organization that was seeking a cure for paralysis. On Wednesday of that week, I received a phone call from an old friend for whom I had raised funds during "The Miracle Walk." I told him all that I had planned.

"I'm very excited for you," he answered. "Maybe I can help you in achieving your goals. Let me call you in a few days about it."

Two days later he called back. "I've made a few phone calls since I talked with you. I have a proposition for you. What if I can find sponsors to pay all your expenses on your row across the country in exchange for using your name to raise funds for paralysis research?" I quickly agreed.

I couldn't believe it. Only four days after our first prayer meeting, all of the expenses were potentially paid for! We met a few times after our conversation to work out the details.

God had answered one of our prayers in four days. But why shouldn't I believe it? God had brought about so many miracles in my life. It was a confirmation that I was right in the middle of His will.

Meanwhile, I was having trouble with the RowCycle. Just days before, I was on a Saturday ride with Steve and Kristi. We were going downhill at over thirty miles per hour. I was flying! All of a sudden, the tension device that kept one of my chains tight, flew off. One end of the chain whipped off of the rear sprocket and flew by my right shoulder. I instinctively withdrew my right arm from the handle barely in time. The chain brushed past the right side of my body and proceeded to wrap around the sprocket with such force that it began to bend one of the cast aluminum bars that held one of the pulleys. My RowCycle started to spin to the right as the right wheel skidded to a stop. It practically threw me out as it came to a standstill up against a curb. Steve and Kristi caught up with me and saw that I was OK but that there was extensive damage to the right side of the RowCycle.

After speaking with a few bike shops, we had no idea about how to fix it. It was time for a modification so this wouldn't happen again. I wasn't as concerned about the safety aspect as I was making the RowCycle more reliable so that breakdowns wouldn't slow us down on the trip. Kristi mentioned the problem to her father, Mack Terry. He seemed to have a few ideas on the subject, so he tried several before developing a dual-direction tensioning system that not only kept the chain tight but lengthened the stroke of the handles. He also put larger sprockets on the rear wheels which effectively reduced the gear ratio, making hills easier to climb. Through trial and error, several other modifications were made. It was rather expensive, but these changes had to be made, or I'd never survive the rigors of the trip. I was moved that Mack would spend hours per day working on the RowCycle when his own business was suffering. Mack is a selfless individual in addition to an engineering genius!

Within one week of our prayer meeting, God had answered two out of five of our prayer needs. Next I spoke with my employers concerning a leave of absence with benefits (insurance for myself and family). My bosses were so excited that they alerted the corporate headquarters in Washington, D.C. Within one week, I was sitting in front of our division president (Chuck Lievrouw) with several other bosses, Steve and Kristi at my side, explaining what the "Row Across America" was all about. After giving him the details he cleared his throat and said: "Rob, I am speaking for the President of DynCorp (Dan Bannister) when I tell you that we are not only behind you 100 percent, but that I have been authorized to continue your entire salary as you row across America for paralysis research!"

I nearly fell out of my chair. I couldn't believe this was happening. God had answered another prayer! He had given me six months of income to cover the six weeks of accelerated training and four months of the trip itself.

The fourth prayer was for health and strength. Both portions of that prayer were about to be answered. One night soon after, I reluctantly agreed to join my wife at a meeting of a vitamin-manufacturing company. I figured it would be a boring meeting. I couldn't have been more wrong! That night a man named Mike talked about his experiences in Vietnam with a chemical called Agent Orange. By the time he was thirty-five, he had already undergone several heart attacks and was dying from the chemical in his bloodstream. He began taking the Shaklee vitamins and proteins. Within months he was almost completely normal and

was on the way to health. I wonde

could give me strength and even mc

kidney infections which had been pl

having serious infections that were

health. I started taking the prescr

weeks, I was stronger and my ir

In addition to the vitamins, I h

on the RowCycle. Soon I was ah

very limit of my strength. I deciu

would row per day on the "Row Across Ame....

told me I was crazy, but I replied that I wanted to choose a gua

genuine miracle so God would receive the credit, not me. Within
months, I was rowing fifty to sixty miles at a clip. But after training on a
daily basis, I developed a pressure sore on my buttocks from the constant
friction of rowing. On each stroke, I did a half situp so the movement of
my hip bones had caused a sore to be rubbed right through my skin.
After a two-week hiatus from training and change of my seating arran-
gemnt, I was off again.

On February 26, 1990, I was able to row from Fort Worth to Dallas
and back in just over twelve hours (5 AM to 5:30 PM). This was approximately seventy miles. Besides the grueling pain of the trip, the highlight
was the beginning. Several of my work mates actually came to the start
point at 5 AM to wish me well. However, I had never been to Fort Worth
City Hall in the dark, and I couldn't find it. After a half-hour search which
included a trip down a one-way street, I chose a point and began rowing.
My work buddies soon found me and led me to the correct location. I
turned to Steve who had been patiently following me through the ordeal
and said, "I sure hope that we can find the Capitol in Washington." Little
did I know that my words were prophetic.

On February 27, I was able to row from Fort Worth to Denton where I
spoke to Texas Women's University. We left at 4 AM and arrived at 8:30.
I was ready for my speech at 10:30. During my delivery to the small
crowd, I mentioned that I was over-training so I would be ready for the
Rocky Mountain and Appalachian ranges. Well, God was about to show
me that He could assimilate the mountains. Steve was riding his bike
beside me when we left Denton for Fort Worth at 1 PM, when we were

an-hour head winds. The wind was so strong that if I
ng downhill, I actually stopped. Normally my average
nd seven miles an hour. My average speed for the thirty-
ure torture was 4.5. Both Steve and I earned every inch of
ack to Fort Worth.

were both exhausted but ecstatic that we could make it under
terrible conditions. Little did we know that we were being prepared
a much greater challenge to come in the months ahead.

I shared my testimony with several churches. It was helpful in preparing me for 100 speaking engagements I would have in 120 days.

One day while training, I crashed going downhill at over thirty miles per hour. This was my most spectacular wreck since training on the Row-Cycle. Even more remarkable, this was the first day in over a year of training that I had forgotten my helmet. I not only rolled the RowCycle, but it actually flipped over. Miraculously, the only damage to me was a fractured hand. Unfortunately, I had wrecked the RowCycle rather badly, and Steve and Mack had to perform major surgery on my machine. As usual, they made the repairs, and I was training once more.

Now with only one month remaining, I averaged forty to fifty miles per day, and it was becoming easier and easier. God had answered four out of five prayers. The fifth prayer concerning Steve's leave of absence was granted, but he would be without income for the four-month trip. In addition Kristi was only able to work sporadically during the year before the trip. Steve and Kristi were completely broke, having only one income. I committed to giving them a percentage of the royalty from *Lord, Lift Me Up . . .*, but this alone was not going to give them the income to pay for their house and other expenses. In addition, we were able to find only one sponsor for the trip, but Wanice and I were thrilled that Fina Oil was going to sponsor about half of the gas expenses. Still, this meant that Wanice and I would have to buy an RV and pay for all of the food for the trip, sinking tens of thousands of our own money into the project. Finally, we also bought at discount large quantities of *Lord, Lift Me Up . . .* to resell along the way. Between my income and the sales of the book (after taking out Steve's royalty percentage), we hoped to pay all the trip expenses. Had we missed God's will in Steve and Kristi coming with me, or was God going to give them income from another source? Even more importantly, had I missed God's will in going on the trip altogether, since almost all of the expenses fell on Wanice and me? Only time would tell.

On the final day of training, Steve and I were planning on traveling over sixty miles. Little did I know my strength was going to be tested uniquely. After going over fifty-four miles and feeling the pangs of pain in my arms, chest, and back, a handicapped friend of mine (whom I had first seen while training several months before) met me on the Fort Worth bike trails. He also had a most unusual three-wheeled vehicle which he used for working out. He pulled up even with me and sized me up for a race which he had been training for over the weeks. Man, he was ready.

"Well, Rob, are you ready for your cross-country trip?" he asked as he rotated two pedal arms with his own huge arms. He had a wild look in his eyes. He was planning on testing my fitness. *But why now?* I thought. *He's fresh and I'm exhausted!* He slowly pulled out ahead just to tease me, then looked back at me with a smile.

"Care for a little race?" he asked, pulling out even more.

"I suppose so," I replied, realizing that I could not beat him in a burst of energy, but would have to outlast him in a test of endurance. So I didn't speed up. I just nodded to him, and he was off and running. Within minutes he was at least a hundred yards ahead. I picked up the pace a little and hoped that I could maintain this new pace. I was incredibly tired after having rowed since early morning. It was now a test of the heart.

The man who wanted the victory the most was going to win. After about a mile he was beginning to tire, and he began to have a worried look on his face. After two miles I caught him on a hill. Within five miles he was out of sight behind Steve and me. I began to realize that our meeting was not an accident. God was showing me that I was as ready for the "The Row Across America" as I was ever going to be.

The following day, March 23, 1990, I flew to Los Angeles where the trip would begin and stayed with the Petersons. I met a man named Dave. While praying about the trip, he had seen a vision of a huge black demon standing in front of the RowCycle with his hands outstretched to stop it. The demon was laughing as I slowed to a crawl. He appeared to be winning when all of a sudden two large angels, each one larger than the demon, began pushing the RowCycle from behind. The demon was pushed back as the angels began helping me pull on the handles.

"Rob, I don't mean to scare you with this bit of news but hold tight to your faith, read the Scriptures, and begin praying. I realize that you will know when the demon is there. It will happen several times in the form of discouragement and severe challenges."

I thanked Dave for his time and thought about his words. They sounded strange, but somehow I knew he was right.

I also began raising money for paralysis research and selling my book. I spoke to several newspapers, radio stations, local schools (Christian and public), Pleasant Valley Baptist Church (our home church when we lived in California), and to Crossroads Community Church at a men's breakfast. In my spare time I trained on the large steep grades outside of Camarillo, California, and rowed to the ocean several times. On one of those occasions, Jeff Wilson put some Pacific Ocean water in a small container for me. It was my intention to pour that water into the Atlantic Ocean seventeen weeks later. I stared at that water container and wondered if it was possible that I would carry the water to the other side of the continent over 3,300 miles away.

A few days later I met with Joni Eareckson Tada, and she taped my testimony, which was broadcast over 500 radio stations. I also was enabled to see all of my California friends who had helped me through the most difficult time in my life. We were not aware they would be helping me again in the strictest physical and spiritual challenge I had ever faced in ways none of us could hardly believe.

Meanwhile, Steve and Kristi made the long drive from Fort Worth to Los Angeles in three days. Steve led a man to Christ on the CB Radio. He was amazed at the size of the Mojave Desert and the California mountains we were going to have to cross. They also had news for me, news that would alter the entire outcome of the trip.

2

Getting Out of Los Angeles Alive—
The First Step Is the Hardest!

Friday, March 30

Where are they? I wondered. I was sitting outside the Los Angeles Airport where I had been waiting an hour for Wanice's plane to land, or for Steve and Kristi to pull up with the RV, whichever happened first. Had anything gone wrong? I was watching hundreds of cars go by. Even though the RV was big, it was going to be tough to see it in all the traffic. Just then a large vehicle turned the corner. It looked like a traveling billboard. Could it be? Yes, it was my RV. It looked different with reflective stickers all over it. It was tough to miss with the huge letters "ROWING ACROSS AMERICA" and dozens of other sponsor decals on it. Steve parked the RV, and we exchanged hugs and stories. Fifteen minutes later, we picked up Wanice and the boys at their gate; then we were off for Camarillo where we were going to spend a quiet weekend together before the madness began.

Saturday, March 31

Steve and I trained all the next day on the hills of Camarillo. They were tough, and I was awed by the seeming impossibility of ever making it over the Southern Rockies and the Appalachians. In the meantime, Kristi rested all afternoon. I wondered why. She couldn't possibly be tired yet. We would find out shortly.

Wanice and the Petersons packed the RV all day. That evening, the Wilsons threw a party for us. We enjoyed seeing all our old friends. However, one of them, Tom Pettigrew, was going to meet with a tragedy soon after that would cause all of us a profound heartache. After the party, we loaded 1,000 copies of my book, *Lord, Lift Me Up* . . . . My friends kept walking out to the RV with box after box. Poor Steve was sticking them everywhere.

"How many more boxes are there?" he asked with dismay.

"Too many to count," came the reply from someone in the garage where the trail of books began. Finally, the convoy stopped, and Steve breathed a sigh of relief.

Sunday, April 1

After saying good-bye to our friends, Steve, Kristi, Jason, and I drove through Los Angeles to Rancho Los Amigos where the trip was to begin. As we pulled up to the rehabilitation center where I had heard those words, "You'll never walk again," a shiver ran down my spine. Much of the pain and feeling of helplessness returned. I shook it off and tried to remember that I did walk again. I had begun a new life here after overcoming a seemingly impossible situation, so it was only fitting that I start a Guinness World Record here also. After parking the RV outside the 1100 building where we were instructed by the police, I glanced at the sign hanging over the door. It was the morgue.

"Hopefully this sign doesn't represent the level of our success," I kidded Steve and Kristi. All of us were full of nervous energy, so we took a walk around Rancho. On the way to the ward where I had spent over four months, we passed the obstacle course. I pushed my wheelchair through the obstacle course just for old time's sake. I was amazed at how easily I wheeled through and jumped over several obstacles. Not only was I much stronger, but I was rather competent with advanced wheelchair skills. I wheeled out of the course, leaving the ghosts of the past behind. Then I took the four of us through 700 building, and we saw the bed I had been in. I told the paraplegic there he could do almost anything he set his mind to and that faith in God was the key. We then went back to the RV and hit the sack. Jason and I talked for a couple of hours as I tried to make up for the time we would be apart. As we shared our feelings, he said, "Dad, I'm proud of you."

Day 1—Monday, April 2

The four of us woke at 6:30. Steve made one final check of our equipment. Steve was soon finding out that his job was awesome. On a daily basis he would be the first out of bed. He would check the RowCycle, his bike, the RV, drive the RV to the starting point, pull the RowCycle down from its perch (no small task since it weighs seventy-five pounds), pull out all our equipment we were to wear that day, help Kristi with her chores, and then bring the RowCycle around for me to climb into. Afterwards, he would have to ride his bike as far as I could row. At the end of the day, he would have to put everything away again and then drive to our speaking engagement and/or to the next RV park.

Kristi would discover she had an equally difficult task. An average day would consist of making breakfast, driving the RV up ahead to the next break point, preparing lunch, going shopping for food, calling the media and churches, assisting Steve with driving, and then cooking supper. Of the three of us, Kristi had the most assignments. If I included all they did on a daily basis, this book would run 1,000 pages.

The theory: my job was going to consist only of rowing, speaking, eating, and sleeping!

By 8, our friends had come down from Camarillo. Phil Britt, Dave Massengale, and Chet Fassette flew in from my home office and served as a DynCorp send-off committee. By 9, we assembled at the starting point, and I began encouraging the patients. I was excited, yet apprehensive, as the minutes ticked by. My hands were already hurting from the abuse they had absorbed in training, and I hadn't even started yet!
How would they stand 120 days of over one million pounds of pressure per day?

Suddenly, the time was here. My heart began to pound as I looked at my watch. I had trained a year and a half for this moment. Was I ready? Time would tell. I only knew I was prepared as I could be. I repeat: God was going to make up the difference. He always does. I also determined I would not quit, no matter what.

The festivities began outside the Physical Therapy building. Dr. Comar, the hospital director, addressed the small crowd and a few members of the media. I didn't hear a word he said. My mind tapes were replaying the first time I had met Dr. Comar.

I had been lying in a body jacket, paralyzed from the waist down, trying to cope with another day in the hospital with all of my new limitations bearing down on me. But a shining ray of hope would visit my room every morning. I can remember waiting to hear his footsteps sounding in the hall. Soon around the corner would come a little old man with a smile that could brighten up the dreariest of days. It was Dr. Comar for his morning visit and thought for the day.

"Good morning, Rob," Dr. Comar would say.

"Remember, the greatest limitation stems from two words: I can't! Get rid of those words. Say those two words that can change your life: I can!"

We would chat awhile, then he would be off to cheer up someone else. I couldn't believe a man that busy would take time to visit us each morning.

My mind came back to the present. Perhaps his hair was a little greyer, but this was the same Dr. Comar. He gave me words of encouragement that I would carry with me into the greatest challenge of my life.

Dr. Comar stepped down from the podium and was replaced by Armondo Lopez and Susan Miranda from Administration. They wished me luck and Godspeed. Physical Therapy was represented by a therapist named Greg who wished me good luck on behalf of all the therapists. I remembered Greg very well because he taught me to play tennis, basketball, and several other sports, despite the fact that he was a quadriplegic. Finally, I was handed the mike. My speech was very short.

"Thanks for allowing me to begin here at Rancho Los Amigos. Rancho represents a new beginning in my life."

I went on to tell them how far I was attempting to go and that I was raising money for paralysis research, setting a Guinness World Record, and encouraging people that they don't have to give up in the face of adversity. I told them about the level of difficulty of what I was doing. I introduced the DynCorp representatives and concluded by saying:"Lastly, my team will consist of my younger brother Steve, who left his job to be with me, and his wife Kristi. I'm going to make it, because if God gives you a dream, there is no mountain too high. You patients will have to climb your own mountains, but with God's help, anything is possible. See you in Washington D.C. in four months."

I rolled away from the podium, ready to begin the trip. Wanice gave me a good-bye kiss, and the boys each gave me a hug. Just as I was ready to pull on the handles for the very first time, I realized that I had forgotten to say the most important thing. I had forgotten to introduce and thank my wife, family, and friends. How could I have been so selfish as not to mention my very own family? I would lose a lot of sleep about that over the course of the next several weeks. I had even failed to mention that Jeff Wilson would be accompanying me for the first two weeks to get us off to a good start. I was about to grab the microphone and say it then, but the crowd began to yell encouragement. The moment had passed. "The Row Across America" had begun at 10 AM on April 2, 1990.

I pulled on the handles and waved to the crowd. Steve joined in behind. We rounded the corner and headed for Imperial Drive. Kristi and Jeff boarded the RV, and friends jumped in their cars to follow us for awhile. Channel 9 from Los Angeles followed us and asked us questions as we made our way down Imperial toward the first row of mountains. Our friends stopped occasionally along the side of the road and would cheer and shout their support as we passed.

At noon we stopped for lunch at a mall and ate together. I was too excited to eat but knew it was important so I gobbled down a sandwich. After lunch, our friends gave us a sendoff and took Wanice and the boys to the airport. I watched the car disappear over the hill. I wondered if the next time I saw them it would be in victory or defeat.

Now the team had been reduced to six: Jeff and Kristi in the van; Steve, Bruce, and John on bikes; and me.

I started rowing again, and soon we found ourselves at the corner of Imperial Drive and Highway 91. Just before accessing the highway, we read a curious sign. It said: *No Bikes Allowed.* I was shocked! I had been told that if there were no alternate routes we could use the highways. I examined the map. There was no alternate route shown on the map, so we hit Highway 91 and headed east. I wasn't aware that we wouldn't be on this flat, easy-going road for long.

After two miles of noisy trucks and cars we passed a truck weighing station on 91. Suddenly, a booming voice seemingly from the skies yelled at us, "No bikes allowed on the highway! Get those bikes off the highway *now!*"

In less than a minute, a policeman had zoomed out of the truck station, pulled up ahead, and was waiting for us. Steve went over to talk with him.

"Officer, my brother is attempting to row all the way across America, not only raising money for paralysis research, but to set a Guinness World Record. We were told that if there were no alternate routes, we could use the highways."

"Oh, but there is an alternate route," he replied with authority.

I closed my eyes. I knew I did not want to hear what he was about to say. I looked up the canyon walls wondering if the alternate route were up there somewhere.

To my horror, the officer described how to reach the alternate route. He pointed up ahead to the next exit ramp which disappeared high into a mountain canyon.

"You take that exit, then follow it up until coming to a crossroad, take a left and go over the hill over there, until you come to the river, then, follow the river bike path until . . ."

I stopped listening. I did not want to hear anymore. They continued to talk for a minute. Then suddenly the policeman changed his tone of voice and I listened in again.

"I'm going to radio up ahead to the highway patrol. If they see you on this highway, they are going to give you some papers you won't like." The subject was closed and we knew it. He didn't offer to escort us, and we knew not even to ask.

The policeman sat there and watched us as we exited the highway and made our way up the canyon walls. I was pulling on the handles at over ninety pounds per stroke for several hundred times before finally coming to the top of the first hill only to see several more up ahead. I looked way down to the nice level highway below and watched the cars with engines of several hundred horsepower each gliding along with ease.

"They should have built the highway for RowCycles and let the much stronger cars use the canyon roads," I joked with my companions. My next statement would be a standing joke for the remainder of the trip: "Highways are for cars and wimps."

We stopped for a quick snack. My snacks almost always included vitamins (I would take eighty-two a day) and protein provided by one of our sponsors. Because I was burning over 5,000 calories per day, I needed the extra nourishment.

Steve and I compared maps with Jeff. In fifteen minutes we were under way again, but this time my arms were beginning to scream. Within two miles we were on Green River Pike. It was beautiful. The river flowed through the mountains and canyons. Its beauty was almost worth the pain. I was amazed at how much water we were drinking. I had drunk almost six quarts of water and still was awfully thirsty. Sweat was pouring out of me as fast as I could replace it. I tried not to think about the fact that I was going to be in the desert for over 1,200 miles.

After several more hills and canyons we were finally out of the valley and heading for the hills of Riverside. In the meantime, I was having tire trouble. Steve changed my tire twice before finding a tube that would stay inflated. As Steve was working on my tire, I watched him as he toiled away, not complaining or doubting God's plan for his life. Steve had left his job just to be here with me. His only income would be a portion of the royalty of the sales of my book, and half of any love offerings from churches. I sat there amazed at his faith in God's provision for his life. I was unaware that he was harboring a secret that was making his step of faith even more incredible.

Soon we were on Magnolia and entering Riverside. My goal was to cover forty miles per day. I looked down at my odometer, and it read forty-eight miles. I decided to make it an even fifty miles for the day and yelled "Two more miles" to the trio following me. They cheered. Within fifteen minutes of painful determination and endurance that surprised even me, we stopped at fifty miles on the dot in front of Riverside High School. I climbed out of the RowCycle and into my wheelchair that Kristi had waiting for me.

Bruce and John dismounted their bikes for the final time and winced with pain as they massaged their aching bottoms. They asked Steve how he was going to be able to ride a bike across America when they were hurting already.

In order for the trip to be a legitimate Guinness World Record, we had to mark the road with spray paint at the end of the day, and then begin at that mark the following morning. We could not cheat by one inch. Just as Steve was about to mark the road for the first time, an idea came to him.

"Instead of just marking the road with a line, let's spell the name *Jesus* as we go. At the end of each day, we will put down the next letter in the name *Jesus.*"

We all watched as he sprayed a "J" on the road. I had no idea how much impact this was going to have on the trip.

Jeff checked his altimeter. We had gone from 150 feet above sea level to 680 feet the first day.

"Not a bad first day," he exclaimed as he began mentally to break down the average slope and make various mathematical computations that only he understood. He was a graduate of the Naval Academy and was currently a naval engineer. He was the brains of the operation and was along for the first two weeks in order to help all of us fall into the best and most logical routine possible. Besides the obvious reasons, I was not sure why Jeff and I felt so strongly that he needed to be here, but both of us knew it was God's will. We would not fully understand why until 2,200 miles later. It would become painfully obvious.

After saying good-bye to Bruce and John, we drove to San Bernadino to the closest RV Park. It was breathtaking as we watched the sun set over the mountains. After dinner, Steve and I went to the showers. On the way, I turned my wheelchair over, sending my clean towel and toiletries to the ground. Upon climbing back into my chair and making my way to the showers, I found that the showers were not wheelchair accessible. Steve had to help me into the shower before taking his own shower. We would soon discover that precious few shower facilities across America were accessible to me. We would have to be creative.

That night, I started a ritual that I would perform each night. I filled out my log, taped a message to Wanice and the boys, and read at least three chapters of Scripture. Soon, we were all asleep.

3

The Name J-E-S-U-S—
If We Remember His Name, He Will Remember Ours

Day 2—Tuesday, April 3

The alarm went off at 5:30. We would soon fall into a routine of Steve and Kristi doing everything to prepare me for the day while I dressed, ate, and read my Bible. They were tireless in their pursuit to meet the daily requirements of the "Row Across America." Jeff and I were up at 6:30, and Steve drove us to our starting point while we dressed and ate.

We calibrated my odometer. This was important since it was one of the ways we had to prove what we did. Just minutes before finishing, my old friend Jay Racz pulled up to take pictures. Jay and I went back six years to the "Miracle Walk" from Fort Worth to Dallas in 1984. He was working for a Texas paper then. Now, he was employed in Riverside and was excited to be able to cover my next attempted record.

He began to shoot pictures as we proceeded through Riverside. Soon we took a left at the bottom of a hill. Steve and I began climbing up the hill while Jeff and Kristi drove ahead to investigate. Our radios had a two-mile range, and Kristi went out of range talking about the size of the hill. This took its toll psychologically on me. I realized that I would have to row over 500 times per mile, at about 100 pounds per stroke times two miles. This meant that I would be pulling over 100,000 pounds just to go to the point where they had gone out of range.

"Steve, tell Jeff and Kristi that I don't want to know what's ahead unless there's a detour," I said in a discouraged tone.

"You got it," Steve replied with understanding.

I just kept pulling on the handles, stroke by stroke, not worrying about the miles, only that next stroke.

Steve conveyed my message when the RV came into range. They informed us that they would wait at the top for us. It took me over an hour and a half to climb the hill. Jeff informed us that we had now climbed from 680 feet to 1,480 feet in only six-and-a-half miles. My mind was amazed that we had just climbed 800 feet; my body wasn't.

Jay continued to pop up out of ravines and perch himself on top of hills, taking pictures as we struggled along foot by foot.

By 10 AM, the Santa Ana winds began to blow against us at speeds from 10 to 25 MPH. This slowed me down dramatically. Since we were not on the highway as planned, we would be forced to go out of our way over ten miles today.

After lunch at a small post office (that's right), we turned left onto Redwood Avenue and headed toward the badlands. Jeff and Kristi went ahead to scout, and I learned later in the day that she had taken a long nap. *Why is she so tired all the time?* I wondered.

Within an hour, we crossed back over 91. I merely wanted to row onto the highway, but I remembered the police officers's warning. By 2 PM we were beginning to climb up Timateo Canyon in the badlands against the Santa Ana winds that were growing stronger by the hour. It required two-and-a-half hours to climb from 1,480 feet to 2,250 feet in the next ten-and-a-half miles. My right chain spring broke. Steve had it fixed in minutes. We would soon learn that parts of the RowCycle would break down almost daily. Steve was always there to fix it! Finally, after thirty-three miles of sweat and pain, we pulled over the final hill into Beaumont. What we saw excited us tremendously.

"Steve, is that a downhill grade I see?"

"I don't know. I haven't seen one in so long I forgot what they look like," he responded half seriously.

We took a left onto 14th Street, then a left onto Beaumont Avenue. We glided along at over ten miles an hour for the last seven miles finally coming to a stop at forty miles right outside Banning.

Steve and I were totally exhausted. Steve was not working nearly as hard as I. However, he had to carry forty pounds of tools and water with him, as well as helping me all day long. He was my legs. Every time I needed him, he was there.

As we loaded the RV, we collected a few dollars for paralysis research from onlookers. One man gave us his last dollar that he was saving for a cheap bottle of wine. The last thing we did was to spray an "E" on the road—the next letter in the name *Jesus.*

Jeff drove us all the way to Barstow where we were going to spend the night before speaking the next morning. We arrived at a KOA Camp after a glorious California sunset. Tomorrow was going to be a big day as well as starting out with a huge surprise.

Day 3—Wednesday, April 4

Jeff was doing his laundry when I awoke. I could hear Steve and Kristi nervously giggling about something behind my closed curtain. Kristi knocked and said she had my breakfast. They came in and plopped down on Jeff's bed and stared at me with smiles. Both of them sat there waiting for the other to begin when Kristi finally nudged Steve.

"Rob, we have some news for you, and we don't know how you're going to take this. We were going to wait for awhile but thought that you would finally figure it out. Rob, do you know how you are always saying that I am Gideon charging off into battle with a paraplegic brother as his army."

"Yes, I remember saying that at churches," I returned, wondering what this was all about.

"Well, now you can say that I am Gideon charging off into battle with a paraplegic brother and a pregnant wife, too!"

He waited for the words to sink in.

As soon as I fully understood what he was saying, I rattled off about five questions in a row as I gave Kristi a hug and shook Steve's hand.

"What? Are you kidding? What do your parents think about you being on the trip, Kristi? Are you feeling all right? Is this going to affect your ability to do your job?"

They answered my questions one by one and explained that they wanted to keep it from me as long as possible so I would have one less matter to worry about. Suddenly, all of Kristi's naps made sense.

Kristi went on to say, "Women have worked in the fields, come in to have their baby, and then gone back out into the fields the same day. This will not affect my job other than not lifting more than fifty pounds, possible morning sickness, and needing a nap once a day."

As she spoke, I thought about Wanice having Jonathan just thirty days after my injury. That alone could have caused a miscarriage. She not only packed all our things but unpacked all of the boxes and set up our new home in California. Wanice was indeed a tough lady. But she wasn't alone. I thought about my secretary Lana who also had worked up until the time she had her baby. If Kristi was willing to give it a try, so was I. I loved Steve enough to take the chance with them, knowing the pregnancy could interfere with the trip. I had put tens of thousands of dollars of my own money into the trip, but blood is thicker than water. Therefore, if Steve and Kristi were willing to gamble that the trip would not hurt Kristi or the baby, I was willing to gamble that it would not adversely affect the trip. I had no idea what far-reaching consequences the pregnancy would have and the number of lives it would change. The baby was on its first mission trip.

Soon Jeff returned, and we all celebrated. They all told me that everyone except me knew about the pregnancy, even Wanice. Frankly, I was glad they had not told me.

After celebrating for an hour, we drove to Fort Irwin, tucked between great desert mountains. Just outside the gate was a tall pile of hundreds of rocks, carefully painted with insignias of all of the various military groups that had trained there. Driving to the gate, Steve pulled the RowCycle down and I rowed onto the base at 11 for a tour. I was introduced to various DynCorp employees and met with the local press. As I rowed past men and equipment, I was told that this was the largest ground combat-training camp in world. Russian tanks and other types of foreign equipment stood ready at that fort to challenge the combat-training teams. Soon, I arrived at the Mojave Room (officers club) and spoke to the men and women there about commitment and finishing what we start. I shared with them my struggle to walk again.

After autographing books, we drove back to an RV park in Palm Springs. We swam in a pool, saunaed, and prepared for the following day.

Our camp was nestled between two large snow-covered mountains we were going to row between the following day. The entire area was covered with thousands of powerful turbine wind fans that rose above the desert floor like huge flowers. We turned in early knowing that the following day was going to be a tough one (as nine-tenths of them would be!). We prayed that the strong wind would change directions.

We all dreamed about the following day. However, Kristi was going to have a dream that would literally change the outcome of our first week.

Day 4—Thursday, April 5

Jeff woke us up at 5:30 and was driving us to our starting place when Kristi told me something I thought was a joke. "Rob, I had a dream last night that you would be able to row eighty miles today." I thought she was kidding so I laughed.

"No, I'm serious," she continued.

"Boy, between being pregnant and that pickle you ate last night, you were bound to have a weird dream."

She continued to explain her dream while I listened. I did not take any of this to heart, of course, but I listened courteously. I had trained for a year and a half for over 2,200 miles, so I knew my limitations. My record for one day was sixty-four miles and that was in flat Fort Worth where I didn't have to row the next day. Now I was in the mountains of California where I *did* have to row the next day and the day after. It seemed impossible. But the more I listened, the more captivated I became with the idea. Could this have been a dream from God? The more I thought about it, the more I was convinced that I was supposed to row for eighty miles.

I was rowing by 7:15, while Jeff and Kristi went to a fast-food place for our breakfast. They caught up with us in Mesa after climbing a rather steep grade. I was still concerned that I was would have to go out of my way over five miles due to staying off of the highway. After breakfast, we talked about our route because Jeff and Kristi were going to buy gas and work on the RV generator.

But, because of the grandeur of the mountains around us, we were not listening as well as we should have. I told the team that I was changing my route through Palm Springs. I thought they heard me, but I was mistaken. This would have an enormous effect on our morning.

Steve and I began to roll down the hill and suddenly realized that the Palm Springs valley we were heading into was downhill for miles. As a matter a fact, we began averaging sixteen miles per hour for three straight hours.

The desert was brown death for as far as the eye could see until on the horizon we saw a patch of green. Soon we reached the oasis ahead on Route 111. It was Palm Springs and Palm Desert. The two cities were the only colorful views in sight. Everything else, although beautiful in a strange way, was brown and dead. We zoomed along through both scenic towns so quickly that we lost track of time. I realized we had not heard from Jeff and Kristi since breakfast.

I looked down at my odometer. It read fifty miles!

Meanwhile, Jeff and Kristi, having finished their chores, were looking for us. Jeff, being the mathematician he was, tried to figure our location by applying the following formula which would have worked if I was averaging eight miles per hour as usual: 8 MPH X 3.5 hours = 28 miles. Obviously, we were almost twice that far along and not even on the road he was searching. Jeff panicked! Maybe this would be a normal reaction for most people, but not for Jeff. I had known him for over seven years and I had never seen him even upset in the least. After all, he had been to Vietnam, the Naval Academy, and on seas rough enough to make the best sailor squirm.

Jeff began driving at an incredible rate of speed, taking corners so sharply that he even emptied the refrigerator onto the floor. Kristi suggested that while we were training, if she could not find us, it was because we were going faster than usual and suggested they drive on ahead.

Jeff finally took her advice by hopping onto I-10 and headed east, hoping they would pass within radio range long enough to contact us and ascertain our position. Finally, by 11 they did contact us and spotted our location. After one hour of heartache for Jeff, they caught up with us. We held a short meeting to make sure that this did not happen again. After Jeff unloaded his well-deserved frustrations on me, we pressed forward.

We passed a sign that indicated we were back at sea level. A sick feeling came over me. That meant I had to climb back up thousands of feet all over again. As a matter of fact before the downhill was over, we were 183 feet below sea level. I knew I had to climb to almost 6,000 feet before long. I also wondered how many times I would have to go back up after losing altitude on each downhill.

However, I was becoming convinced that Kristi was right about her dream. By this time we had covered fifty-five miles. But I felt threatened by a massive object looming in the distance. It actually seemed to grow taller as we approached. It was Chiraco Summit, as I feared, our first really tough mountain.

Soon we arrived at the point where we could finally go onto the Interstate and head east. However, upon arriving at the entrance, there staring us in the face was the now familiar sign: *No Bikes Allowed.* There was another "encouraging" sign as I looked at Chiraco Summit that disappeared into the sky. It read: *Turn Off Air-Conditioner So Engine Does Not Overheat.*

How long is this mountain? I wondered. The mountain was placed there many centuries ago as the earth was being formed by God. Now the question was: Who was going to win the victory today—the mountain or me?

By this time we had already gone out of our way over fifteen miles in the first three days. What now? We examined our maps and saw that there were no alternate routes. We asked one of the locals, and he directed us back to Route 111 and Route 195 that would lead us to Box Canyon Road. We stopped at 1 PM for lunch after rowing sixty-three miles. We rested under pine trees attractively situated between Chiraco Summit to the east and the Brown Mountains to the south. As I looked behind us, the two snow-covered mountains, together called Devil's Gate, were only a memory and barely visible on the horizon.

Steve was sunburned, and we both had sun poisoning which had developed into bright red bumps. As Kristi served us a bountiful lunch, we talked and contemplated our afternoon route. Any way we figured, we were going to have to go over Chiraco Summit. Even more importantly, if I were going to fulfill the prophecy of Kristi's dream, I still faced seventeen miles up the biggest mountain I had ever attempted. Even though the first part of the day had been predominantly downhill, it had still taken its toll on me. I was tired! As you travel with us, maybe you will actually empathize with that constant fatigue.

Steve's sunburn was doctored, and he placed protective coverings on his legs. We left at 2 PM, and I pointed the RowCycle toward the summit. The first few miles were uphill but at a small grade. Soon we were in the canyon, and the grade steepened to around 7 percent. However, the great thing about Box Canyon was that I could see only about a half a mile ahead. The road ahead would disappear to the right or the left. I did not have to look seventeen miles up like it would have required if I had been permitted onto the Interstate. A Voice in my heart said, "Don't worry about the next seventeen miles. You can go half a mile, can't you?"

I would sometimes answer verbally, "Yes, Lord, I can go half a mile."

That's how I continued through Box Canyon, a half mile at a time. At times, even that was too great a chore, and I would just concentrate on the next stroke. I began drinking a quart of water every other mile. I pulled stroke after stroke, mile after mile. I almost became comatose trying to escape the torture I was putting my body through.

I was jolted back to reality when a large lizard crawled across the road. Now I was fading in and out of consciousness as my heart raced and my muscles screamed. I began to sing, "Angels, We Have Heard on High." When I reached the part about the mountains "echoing their joyous strains," I got the impression that the mountains themselves were rooting for me. I was only semi-conscious as I watched the miles go by— seventy-five, seventy-six, seventy-seven. An eagle was soaring overhead. I watched as he effortlessly followed the wind currents that carried him along. How I wished that my path over the mountain was as easy. The miles continued to pass, but much more slowly. My average speed was 3 to 4 miles per hour. I watched my odometer with growing excitement. Could it be done? My arms, back, and stomach cried out for me to stop this madness, but I couldn't.

Gradually, I realized that this mountain was only a hunk of rock without a soul. I not only had a soul, but God was on my side. *And if God be for us, who can be against us?* I thought. Looking at my odometer after each half-mile stretch of road, it read: 78, 78.5, 79, 79.5, 79.9. Steve went ahead to mark the spot, so I would have a clear stopping point. I knew if I stopped short, I would never be able to start again. Suddenly a chain broke. Immediately my muscles began to freeze up on me. The mountains seemed to laugh at me as I came just one tenth of a mile from my goal. Knowing that I could not wait for Steve to fix the chain, I began pushing on the wheels. The mountains stopped laughing. Ten more pushes on the wheels, nine more, eight more. My body could not go on, but it did. Five more, four, three, two! With a great surge of energy in my arms, I pushed one last time.

Jeff, Kristi, and Steve erupted into cheers as we saw Kristi's dream come true. My surroundings seemed almost surreal as my senses began to come back to me. I cheered as best I could, barely able to raise my arms at all. But what was that noise? I looked all around and then straight up. They were power lines! I heard the power zipping through the wires, when suddenly I heard that Voice in my heart again.

"Rob, you got power from on high to do this. You tell all those churches about this day. Don't you ever dare take credit for this. Tell them that I did this. You keep spelling My Son's name, and you'll make it. You stop, and I'll take My hand off you. It will be over."

After having a time of prayer, we sprayed down the next letter of the name of *Jesus*—a big "S." Checking the altimeter, we had climbed from 183 feet *below* sea level to 1,425 feet *above* in just twelve miles.

I was ready for a gigantic meal. We drove back to Indio where we stayed at one of the most beautiful RV Parks I had ever seen. It was another oasis in the desert. Even though I was paying the bills, and this was an expensive place, I was ready to celebrate. After eating a multi-course meal, I relaxed in a hot tub. After making a few phone calls and reading my Bible, I was fast asleep and dreaming about the following day. I was secretly praying that no one would dream about how many miles I was supposed to go. Happily, no more dreams of this kind were to visit us on the trip. However, as I was to learn, there was an important reason for rowing the eighty miles that day.

Day 5—Friday, April 6

I was rowing by 8:15 AM. A real miracle had occurred as I slept: I was not sore, but I was dead tired. Within the next hour, we climbed 200 more feet and were finally over Chiraco Summit. A rare phenomenon was in the sky—clouds. This was most unusual for the desert. After four days, we were finally allowed on I-10. We began gliding along at eight to nine miles an hour. We were not used to the traffic noise, but soon our senses were dulled, and we barely noticed it. During the next several hours we would descend from 1,600 feet to 600 feet. We stopped in

Twenty-nine Palms for lunch and were joined by a large motorcycle gang. While we were talking with the gang, a delivery truck pulled up.

"Are you Rob Bryant?" the driver asked.

I couldn't believe that they delivered packages on the road, but I answered yes.

"Well, praise God! My name is Duane from the First Southern Baptist Church in Brawley where you will be speaking Sunday."

We talked for a moment before he had to leave. After lunch we were back on the interstate, and the hours passed quickly.

The desert here was flat and brown. The shoulder of the road had just been repaved so our tires were throwing tar and pebbles at us. Later in the afternoon, my seat clamp broke and my chain fell off five times. Each time, Steve would have me going in minutes. At around 3 PM something brown was in the air up ahead, but we couldn't tell what it was. We grew closer when suddenly we could see what it was—a cloud of bugs and gnats. They went into our mouths, noses, and ears. Extra protein! We kept going as quickly as possible and were out of the swarm in minutes.

Steve began picking up change on the highway. He figured that he was out of work, and a dollar of change per day would be over $100 by the trip's end. I would be talking to Steve and suddenly he would stop. Glancing in my mirror, I would see him picking up change or tools.

Soon we had covered our forty miles, and we stopped for the day in Desert Center. I was thankful for a day of travel on flat terrain. We sprayed a "U" on the road and drove to a lovely RV park in Blythe beside the Colorado River.

Day 6—Saturday, April 7

The team was functioning like clockwork as everyone did their jobs. Now it was my turn all too soon. I was rowing by 7:30 AM, always sore and tired. I was discouraged about my hands. They were getting worse by the day. Could they make it? On an average day, I would pull and squeeze on the handles 18,000 to 20,000 times.

Trucks began honking their horns and police turned on their lights as the news of our trip began to spread. It was another hot, dry day. Our altitude changed by only a few hundred feet all day.

Steve found a wallet beside the road and gave it to Jeff for safekeeping until we could turn it in. I was amazed that Steve did not rationalize that God had given him some income because he was out of work. Within minutes a man pulled him over and asked Steve if he had seen it. Steve immediately radioed Jeff and instructed the man to go get it from our RV. We wondered later if we were being tested by the enemy.

Soon we passed the Blythe Airport and could see the city and riverbanks ahead. We received directions from the local police and knew how we must go through Blythe and across the large bridge over the Colorado River. By 2:30 PM, we found ourselves crossing the river, and we were on the Arizona side of Blythe. We had traversed our first state! I tried not to think about the fact that I had twelve more to go. We stopped by 3 PM for the day. We were putting the "S" down when a revelation hit me. The trip across California was supposed to take seven days. It took only five. In other words, the name *JESUS*, five letters, carried us across California. Suddenly I remembered what the Voice had said.

"Rob, you got power from on high to do this. You tell all of those churches out there about this day. Tell them that I did this. You keep spelling My Son's name, and you'll make it. You stop and I'll take My hand off you. It will be over." I shared the revelation with the team as they busied themselves for a long drive.

Jeff drove us to El Centro to our first church of the trip on the following morning. We met the pastor, Jonathan Morgan, and his family at his home. I stayed nearby in the home of a member named Ina Ray. Jeff stayed at the Morgan's, and Steve and Kristi spent the night at Barbara's house. That night, we ate at a school function. I consumed twelve pieces of meat and three plates of other food. I was losing weight and could not find enough to eat. I spoke to the school briefly concerning my struggle to walk again and what I was doing now. Kristi and Steve were absent because Kristi was having her first bout with sickness.

The first week of the trip was over. I had learned a great deal not only about the difficulties of the trip, but about God's provisions for us. One week down, sixteen to go!

4

The High Desert—
How Much Do We Want to Succeed?

Day 7—Sunday, April 8

I shared my testimony and toward the end made this statement: "If God is for us, there is no power that can stop us."

I knew that God had given me the words. I also knew that voicing this idea challenged hell itself. I would continue saying this to every church. I would not have to wait long for the fulfillment of such a bold claim.

At the close of my testimony, several people came forward. Pastor Morgan felt it was the best service since he had come to the church. After the service, CBS Sports came to interview us. It was our first of many TV appearances from a church.

We ate lunch with the Morgans and drove to El Centro to speak at Central Baptist Church. On the way, the desert changed from brown to stark white sand dunes. Motorcycles and dune buggies filled the desert floor. We watched them for a moment before moving on.

I spoke during the service. A girl who had recently tried to commit suicide stepped out to recommit her life. After the close of the service I spoke with a woman who had something strange to say. She looked around as if to see if anyone were listening. "I saw a light emanating from your body as you spoke," she said quietly. I dismissed the comment figuring that she was a believer in light energies and auras, but the pastor explained that this comment was very out of character for her.

The pastor was to have heart surgery the next week so we prayed together. We would find that almost all of seventy-six churches we were to speak to were hurting in one way or another and needed to hear what God had to say through me.

Unintentionally, I left my Bible in the pulpit. I would have to rewrite all of my notes and do without my favorite Bible until it caught up with us in West Texas.

I have been told after taking IQ tests that I have an above-average IQ. However, my wife will tell you that I would lose my head if it were not screwed on. This phenomenon was made worse by the extreme fatigue I experienced on a daily basis. Steve and Kristi had their hands full doing their own jobs at speaking engagements. Keeping track of my Bible was my job. I did not do especially well.

Jeff drove us back to Blythe. The three of us tried to sleep en route but found it difficult due to the hills and sharp curves on the small desert roads. We arrived at 1 AM. We slept on the side of the road in order to save time and money. I checked my money. It was almost gone! Between the food, gas, Steve and Kristi's portion of the book sales, and other expenses, I was almost broke. The trip was far more expensive than I had thought. I had more money back home, but it was our life savings, and I hated to touch it. I prayed for God's help with my finances. I marveled at Steve's faith concerning money. I would learn many lessons from my younger brother. As with Joseph, the younger brother was the older brother's teacher.

Day 8—Monday, April 9

I began rowing at 8:45 AM at the Arizona border. What a way to begin a week! I had to row twenty-five miles uphill. Our ascent began at 400 feet elevation beside the river. We passed Quartzsite and made our way through Granite Pass to an altitude of 1,925 feet. I wanted to go the distance without stopping to test my strength in the heat and mountains of the desert. I had 1,000 more miles of desert. I needed to know where the boundary of my stamina was. We had covered twenty-six miles by lunch. After lunch the terrain leveled, and we were able to go over forty-eight miles before stopping for the day.

We were less than 100 miles from Phoenix now, but the desert was taking its toll on Steve and me. We were burned and exhausted. My arms and Steve's hips were sore.

After finishing for the day, we drove to the town of Vicksburg which appeared on all of our maps. It consisted of three buildings: one house, one store, and a barn. That was it! We finally found an RV park in Quartzsite called Black Rock. The name fit it well. The entire ground was covered with igneous rock that was as black as coal with occasional streaks of brown. As barren as it was, it was still gorgeous. I thought of Wanice as nightfall filled the canyon and the moon rose high above the black rock around us. I began to miss her more and more. A friend drove out from L.A. to see us. He had driven the 300 miles we had just crossed and marveled at the accomplishment thus far.

Later that night I took a bath outside of the RV in my wheelchair because of a lack of bathrooms. I had waited until dark to do this for privacy's sake and thought I was alone. Upon turning around to dry off, I saw an older couple sitting outside their RV watching me as I bathed. I laughed, figuring I had shocked them as much as they had shocked me.

Day 9—Tuesday, April 10

Along the way to our start point, we saw a coyote running across the desert floor. I wondered how any living thing could survive here. Both Steve's and my skin were dry and slightly burned, but Jeff found a cure for that later in the day.

I began rowing at 8:45 after reading Romans 8:14-20 to the team. The crux of the message was that our present suffering wasn't anything compared to what was waiting for us in heaven. I clung to those Scriptures and repeated them over and over as I continued my trek across the desert. I was very tired now but, amazingly enough, not sore. We scanned the horizon and saw nothing but brown shades of sand and igneous rock. After lunch Kristi made a startling discovery. An important bit of data had eluded the team.

"We forgot to check our gas gauge. We're down below one tenth of a tank," Kristi reported.

We looked around. We were in the middle of nowhere. There was no sign of civilization in sight. After checking the map for the next off ramp, our hearts sank. There was no sign of a town on our maps.

"OK, there is no reason to panic," I said, knowing what a ridiculous statement I had just made.

"Just start driving east. If you run out of gas, we will pass you and go find help."

I was already tired. I wondered how many miles I would have to row with Steve to find help. I could have suggested that Steve go ahead by himself if the need arose because he was so much faster than I. But if he ran into trouble by himself in the desert, the results could have been fatal.

No one had a better idea. After Steve secured extra water for us, they pointed the RV east and disappeared over the hill. Steve and I began wondering how far they would go. After a few miles, the van reappeared with two smiling faces on board. They had driven only four miles to Tonopah for gas. Soon, we passed the exit. Sure enough, there was an exit with a lone gas station.

We stopped for the day at 4 PM after rowing forty-one miles. I ate four plates of food. I ate enough for an army platoon.

During the day, Jeff had sewn sleeves on our T-shirts for extra protection from the sun. I took a shower at the park in a wheelchair-accessible shower that was a big open room like a gym. This was my first easy shower on the trip. As I crawled into bed with my very tired body begging for sleep, I noticed how much weight I had lost thus far. There were no scales around so I was not sure how much I had lost. As I went to sleep I fought the fear of failure or running out of water. At least once I had dreamed of running out of water on a deserted stretch of desert road. I fought back with Scriptures and confidence that I was doing the right thing.

Day 10—Wednesday, April 11

I read Scriptures from Romans concerning the strong lifting up the weak. As a team, we all had strong and weak points. I explained that we needed to help the others with our strong points.

With my hands sore and stiff, we began our day as usual, and I was rowing by 8:15 AM. I wondered if I were developing arthritis.

It was a boring row day, mostly flat with a smattering of slight hills. However, I was being slowed down once again with head winds. Since Steve and I were not battling mountains as usual, we had plenty of time to talk.

"Steve, the part of my testimony at churches that I am not comfortable with is the closing. I just kind of stop talking and then turn it over to the pastor. I need an invitation statement."

As he was thinking about it, the Voice in my heart simply suggested, "Spell My name."

I began thinking of the name *JESUS*. Suddenly I saw the name as an acronym.

"Steve, has God revealed anything to you that begins with the letter J?"

"Yes. Joy!" he responded with a smile.

Between the two of us we selected adjectives or verbs that spelled out the name of Jesus.

We said that "J" stood for Joy. After you are saved you are filled with joy. "E" stood for excellence. After being saved we need to move on to excellence. "S" stood for sacrifice. When we sprayed down the "S" on the third day of the trip, we knew we had sacrificed. But God will never ask you to sacrifice more than His Son did on the cross for us. "U" stood for unyielding. We need to be unyielding to sin. And the final "S" in the name Jesus stood for supernatural. If our lives could be explained by our own gifts or talents, we would receive the glory. Yet, if something happens in our lives that has no other explanation but God, then He and He alone receives the glory.

It was so powerful, yet simple, that we were convinced it had come from God. I would use it during the invitation for the remainder of the trip.

Meanwhile, our friends back home in Texas were being hit by torrential downpours, causing wide areas of flooding and record-high water levels. What I learned was that their weather was so severe it turned the winds around out here in the desert. So, instead of prevailing westerly winds as normal, they were out of the east as each low pressure area passed by us in a rush. It was a another hot, dry day filled with more lizards.

At lunch both Steve and I had the stomachache. Mine was not bad, but Steve was nearly doubled over in pain. He didn't complain. Later that day I noticed something shiny on my pant legs. Upon looking down and focusing on the object, I saw a needle and thread sticking out of my pants. Since I could not feel from the waist down, I prayed that it was not sticking out of my leg. I was fortunate. It was merely lying there. Later I learned that after Jeff had finished sewing sleeves on my T-shirts, he could not find the needle. I did!

As we approached Phoenix, our surroundings slowly became more agricultural. Steve and I watched as the farmers plowed their dry fields. It was so dry and dusty that plowing caused dust to go hundreds of feet into the air.

The media on the trip thus far had been light because we were out in the middle of the desert. However, I was informed that the footage shot in L.A. as we left had been shown in Germany as well.

We finished for the day at over forty-three miles. We drove to Good-year, Arizona, outside Phoenix, to an RV park. The Indian-style buildings were a work of art. After swimming in a large pool and bathing in a comfortable shower, we turned in early, preparing for another busy day.

Day 11—Thursday, April 12

We took the day off to fix the RV generator. Kristi said she badly needed the air-conditioner in her condition. Steve and Jeff drove to North Phoenix at 8 AM while Kristi and I swam, relaxed, and watched movies in the restaurant. With a real day off to rest, I had time to think about how much I missed my family. This was the first year that I was not coaching Little League Baseball with my boys. I felt like I was being selfish in not being with them.

In order to give Kristi a real day off from her duties, I called the media and upcoming churches that weekend. Steve and Jeff returned from Phoenix, and we rested the remainder of the day. Praise the Lord for rest. One old Gospel song goes, "I'm gonna sit down beside my Jesus, Gonna sit down and rest a little while." Amen!

Day 12 — Friday, April 13

I had four speaking engagements; two radio phone interviews, one in-studio interview with KFLR in Phoenix, and one at the DynCorp installation in Phoenix, with several miles between each. I was forced to take another day off. I was deeply discouraged about resting two days in a row, but our schedule did not permit otherwise. After the three radio station interviews, we went to DynAir at the Phoenix Airport. After meeting several of the men personally, I was raised high into the air on a platform. I addressed the men and women as a fellow DynCorp employee, explained what I was doing, and challenged them never to give up in the face of adversity.

Neither of the four of us could believe that we had almost completed two weeks on the "Row Across America." Mentally, it seemed like it had just begun. Physically, it felt more like an eternity. Nevertheless, it meant that we had to say good-bye to Jeff. He would be leaving the next morning as we passed the Phoenix Airport. Jeff and I talked for over an hour about our strategy now that the team was being reduced to three. As he talked I thought about what a paradox this man was. He was so busy with his own career and family, yet had flown to Fort Worth to help me walk from Fort Worth to Dallas six years before. Now he had just given up two hard-earned weeks of vacation for me. Jeff always seemed to know what was important and what to devote his time to. I envied this man for his calm spirit. Other than the obvious reasons, we still did not know why it was so vital for Jeff to be on the trip. It would be revealed much later.

I began to claim a promise that my pastor Hal Brooks had shared from the pulpit just before he died after a painful struggle against bone cancer: "We should never doubt in the darkness what God has shown us in the light." In the days to come, dark times were to surround all three of us like a shroud.

We were all asleep by 9, so we would be ready to get on the road again.

5

Christt Is the Living Water—
He Is Sufficient for Every Need

Day 13—Saturday, April 14

I was awakened by the singing of "Happy Birthday." I was so busy that I had forgotten. But Steve and Kristi remembered. Kristi felt too ill to cook and picked up breakfast from a fast-food place. We began rowing by 7:15. While we rowed, Kristi took Jeff to the airport. Returning, she could not find us along the prearranged route because we could not row on I-10. We were nearing downtown Phoenix when we heard Kristi on the radio. Minutes later she found us. She fixed us lunch. While we ate, the *Phoenix Gazette* took our picture and interviewed us.

Steve and I proceeded down city streets through East Phoenix and were soon back out in the desert. Slowly the minutes merged into hours. The sun was high overhead, and the temperature climbed to over ninety. Steve and I began to worry about Kristi. We got back on I-10 about fifteen miles out of Phoenix. Steve spray painted large arrows on the road showing Kristi where we had accessed the interstate. We checked our water supply. We were down to less than a quart—total. Where was she? Within another hour, we were down to one gulp of water apiece. Suddenly, we heard her on the radio.

"I see you. I'm about to pass. Everything OK?"

"Yes, we're OK, but we need you to stop at the next exit."

Even though we were low on water, we could make it to the next exit. We could see the next two exits up ahead. We were within a mile of them. We had made it. We both drank our last bit of water.

Kristi drove ahead. I looked at my odometer. It read forty-one miles. We could stop for the day at the next exit. We watched her pass the first exit. She didn't turn off. Why? We moved ahead, figuring she had used the second exit for some reason. Approaching the first exit, we felt a little sick. It was an overpass, not an exit. We looked ahead. The second exit was also an overpass. Steve called Kristi on the radio. There was no answer. She was over two miles away, out of range.

All right, don't panic, I said to myself. *The next exit can't be far.* But how much farther could we go without water?

Don't think, just row, I told myself.

Steve and I didn't talk—we just watched for the next exit as we started again. Since I knew I was out of water, and sweating heavily, I became even thirstier.

Finally we passed the first overpass. We looked for the next exit. The road disappeared into the horizon. All we saw was brown sand and mountains. We looked at each other then back at the road.

We went ahead not talking, knowing that we had to save even the moisture in our mouths. Between the two overpasses we saw a sign. It read: *Gas and Lodging Next Exit—8 MILES.*

I hoped we were not hallucinating in the desert sun. The words jumped out at us: 8 MILES!

We stopped under the next overpass. Steve said, "I'm sure that Kristi read this sign and is on her way back."

"That's true, but if she isn't, we're in real trouble. We're going to have to move ahead. If she does come back, she'll see us from the other side and come back. Besides, she doesn't know we're out of water!"

That's when the Voice in my heart rang out, "Christ is the living water." I shared the verse with Steve, and we pressed on. Before long our sweating slowed. Our bodies began running out of water. Soon my throat was too dry to talk. I tried not to look at my surroundings. It only served to make me thirstier. Slowly my energy level began dropping. Within another mile my average speed was only six. At this speed we would reach Kristi in another hour. We normally drank a quart or more of water per hour. The desert air sucked the moisture right out of our bodies. Slowly, the miles passed. I began slipping in and out of reality.

"Rob, there it is," Steve cried with a raspy voice.

Up ahead I could make out the next exit. Steve got on his radio immediately. "Kristi, we are out of water and sunburned. Get two quarts of water and wet washclothes ready for us."

Suddenly I had a burst of power. My average speed picked up to eight and nine again, and I exited the interstate. We saw the RV in the distance. My odometer read 49.6 miles for the day. As we were ready to leave, a policeman pulled up.

"What are you doing?" he asked politely yet with authority. I told him.

"I hate to tell you this, but you can't use the interstate between here and Tucson. There is an alternate route through the Indian reservation on the west side of the freeway. It will take you all the way to Tucson." Then he paused and thought a minute.

"How fast does that thing go?" he asked.

Steve answered, "about eight miles per hour."

"Huh, eight miles per hour? Tell you what. Just stay on the interstate. If anyone says anything, show them this."

He reached into his pocket and gave us one of his cards. We thanked him and then he left. Steve loaded the RV and we headed back to Phoenix to a waiting motel, courtesy of Southside Baptist Church.

After we cleaned up, Steve suggested we ought to go shopping. So we drove for half an hour as he looked for the right spot. I looked out of the window. We were soon sitting outside an Italian restaurant. Kristi went in, and Steve helped me with my wheelchair.

"What gives?" I asked.

"Shut up. It's your birthday, isn't it?"

I couldn't believe it. Steve and Kristi were almost broke, yet they were taking me out to eat at an expensive restaurant. I marveled at their faith in God's provision for them.

We ate a gourmet meal, but Kristi was too sick really to enjoy it.

There was only one motel room reserved for us, so I gave it to Steve and Kristi. I was too tired to care. In a few minutes I was asleep in the RV.

Day 14—Sunday, April 15

On Sunday morning we slept until 8:30. Kristi was too ill to go to church or eat, so Steve and I went. Trouble continued as we drove into the Southside Baptist Church parking lot where I was to speak to the youth. Steve judged that we could get under their overhang and tore a gaping hole in the RV roof, ripping off the top of the luggage rack. This hole was going to allow water to seep into boxes of books below.

I spoke to the youth. Steve later told he thought it was the best presentation I had made to date. We ate with the youth minister, Danny Kuykendall, and his family. Kristi was again too sick to eat and stayed in the RV. After an enjoyable visit with the Kuykendalls, we drove to West Phoenix Baptist Church.

It was the first night of revival at the church. Later that week, they were to have a football player and other guest speakers. When I gave the invitation, about one fifth of the church came forward. Several people decided for salvation, as well as other decisions. Two men even prayed for deliverance from homosexuality. It was an incredible service!

However, since neither the pastor nor I mentioned the book, we sold only four copies. I was in financial trouble. I was hoping that the book would pay for our daily expenses. Satan tried to depress me, but I tried to remember what the trip was all about: raising money for paralysis research, setting a Guinness World Record, and, most importantly, sharing with God's people that if God was for us, there was no power that could stop us. There we hooked up the RV to the church's power. After everyone had left, the RV evidently overloaded the circuit when Steve turned on the microwave. We ate a cold meal for supper. Within an hour the RV began to become mighty hot, and we sweat like crazy. We slept only a couple of hours in the stale interior heat of the RV. Once again, I had left my Bible inside a church with all my notes inside it. Voices of darkness plagued me all night.

Day 15—Monday, April 16

Steve fixed our breakfast, and we were rowing by 7 AM. Despite Kristi feeling sick, she lined up speaking engagements at the University of Arizona in Tucson on Wednesday, and confirmed speaking to Williams Air Force Base on Tuesday. Meanwhile, Steve and I were facing our own challenges. We were heading south to Tucson on I-10 with head winds of fifteen to thirty miles per hour. The grade was gentle, but we had a 500-foot climb throughout the day. A seat clamp broke, and as always, Steve had me going again in minutes. After lunch and another couple of hours of rowing into the wind, we stopped at 3 PM for the day at forty-one miles. That night at the RV park, Steve fixed the generator that had not worked since hooking up to the church the night before. Once again the showers were not accessible, so Steve brought me warm water from the RV, and I washed outside in my wheelchair in the cool night air. The wind continued to blow, so it was a bath to remember.

Day 16—Tuesday, April 17

Kristi continued not to sleep well. We all slept in till 9. Steve drove us back to Phoenix, and I spoke to DynCorp employees at Williams Air Force Base, after which I actually rowed across the flight line. It was a tremendous amount of fun rowing past all of the aircraft. I asked a few of the pilots if they wanted to race. I spoke to at least fifty DynCorp mechanics in a hangar. I spoke from the RowCycle and told them what I was doing. I urged them never to give up on their dreams, regardless of the cost. We ate a tremendous lunch at the officers club with Janet Cooperman, Joe Young (division manager), and Doug Monroe. Kristi felt better and ate more than she had in days. Kristi and I were both losing too much weight.

After leaving Williams AFB, Steve drove us back to our starting point. We began rowing at 5 PM. This was our first evening to row, so it was a pleasant change from the blistering heat. The wind continued to blow at fifteen to twenty-five miles per hour out of the south. After an hour the air began to cool. Steve and I put on jackets for the first time on the trip. As the evening wore on, a few lizards and snakes came out to feed one last time before nightfall.

We climbed another 500 feet to reach an altitude 2,100 feet. This gradual upgrade combined with the direct head wind caused each stroke to require from seventy to ninety pounds. As nightfall approached, I hit my arms on the wheels several times, making them bleed. We watched a spectacular sunset at around 6:30. We had one eye on the road and one eye on the brightly colored horizon to our right. Steve and I battled against the wind, cold, and darkness until 8:45 PM. We finished with only twenty miles for the day.

Day 17—Wednesday, April 18

Since the RV park did not have hook-ups, we spent an evening with the windows open. It was a cool night so it was comfortable, but we were right beside the interstate so it was noisy. No longer able to sleep, I awoke at 5:30. During the ensuing hour, I prayed for our entry into Tucson that day. The sunrise was overwhelming. I realized I had also watched the sunset the night before while rowing. So tired!

We were rowing by 7 AM. Our goal was to row twenty-four miles into Tucson on I-10. Once again we had five- to fifteen-mile-per-hour head winds and an uphill struggle. We had to climb from 2,100 feet to 2,700 feet. The hours slowly passed. As we approached Tucson, we looked for an exit that had an alternate route. Not finding one, we went all the way into Tucson on the shoulder of I-10. The traffic became heavy and scared Steve and me. Soon we would be facing a much more dangerous traffic situation.

We finally exited, rowed right into downtown Tucson, and ate at a fast-food place. From there we rowed to the University of Arizona. We were met by Pastor Johnson of 22nd Street Baptist Church. I was led to the Baptist Student Union building where I spoke to the students about commitment and shared my testimony. I was amazed at the size of the university. I was even more amazed that out of 36,000 students, only fifty came to BSU. After speaking, I ate a large helping of spaghetti with the students. This was my second lunch within an hour; I wasn't complaining.

NBC, Channel 4, came out to the university and filmed a rather lengthy interview. The pastor led us to our hotel, so we could prepare for the service that evening at his church. We had two rooms; it was great. Once again Kristi was too sick to attend church. Steve and I ate at the church, and then I spoke. I felt it was the best service of the trip so far, and I was becoming less dependent on any notes.

Day 18—Thursday, April 19

Steve and I met for breakfast at 5:30. Kristi felt ill and slept in.

Steve and I started rowing at 7 and took Broadway to Old Spanish Trail to Houghton and then up a long hill out of Tucson. Steve and I turned and looked back behind us. We could look down on the city of Tucson. The desert completely surrounded the city and swallowed it up. As far as we could see in every direction was brown sand and mountains. It was strangely lovely, yet an ominous sight when rowing hill by hill and hour by hour.

I began rowing again. A thought suddenly jolted me.

"Steve, we forgot to pray this morning!"

"Yes, you're right," he returned with an urgent tone.

While we were praying, a big Cadillac pulled up and stopped ahead of us. We finished our prayer just as a friendly looking man stepped out of the car and walked back to us.

"Hi, my name is Fred Ruth. I saw you guys on television last night. I own a car dealership over in Benson, just east of here. If there is anything I can do for you in the way of car repair, I'll do it for free. I really admire what you're doing."

Steve and I sat there dumbfounded. One of our prayer requests just moments ago was about the RV damage. I cleared my throat.

"Well, there is just one thing . . ." I went on to explain about the damage to the RV. Ruth assured us that there would be no problem in fixing it and to stop in later that day.

We shook hands, and he drove away. Was it only a coincidence that he drove by just after we prayed and that he lived in the next town we were passing through? I did not think so!

I began rowing again as we both voiced our praises to God for sending Fred Ruth to us.

Within several miles we accessed I-10 again as Kristi passed us. I was glad that she had had the opportunity to sleep in.

We began our climb to Benson—from 2,600 feet to 3,800 feet. By 9 AM, we started to climb a fifteen-mile-long hill. I was amazed that I did not stop one time in the ascent. For the first time in one week we had a tail wind. It was out of the west! Yeah, we had lunch. By 12:20, I was rowing again and finished the hill while Kristi drove the RV To Fred Ruth's dealership.

Now at the top of the hill we looked down to Benson below. The desert mountains consumed everything in sight. It was awe-inspiring, but we realized how completely surrounded by the desert we were. The downhill grade we were looking at was seven miles long and one of the steepest of the trip. I reached a speed of thirty-six. I should have been excited as the miles zoomed by, but I was busy looking at the other side of the valley. For every mile I was going down, I would have to go back up. As a matter of fact, we had dropped below the altitude where we had started in the morning.

As we passed through Benson, the interstate leveled off for several miles. Glancing at my odometer, I was already past our daily goal of forty miles. Meanwhile, Kristi was getting the RV fixed and had some wonderful news for us. We had plenty of water so we planned on continuing to row until Kristi's return. We passed close enough to tell Kristi by radio of our plans and started our ascent up the next mountain.

This was just like the other side of the valley—sternly steep and long. I could row only a hundred yards or more before stopping in utter exhaustion. I even had to push on the wheels! I figured that I was pulling 100 pounds per stroke for the first time on the trip. I continued to push on the wheels and pull on the handles until the pain was so intense, I cried. Steve shouted a word of encouragement. We reached the first plateau of the hill and finished for the day. I could go no further. The first part of the hill had been two-and-a-half miles. I finished the day at fifty-three miles. I looked up the mountain from my vantage point and could not see the top.

Let tomorrow take care of itself, I thought.

We waited for an hour and drank a milkshake together. Suddenly we heard Kristi on the radio. We learned later that because of our lofty position on the mountain, we were talking to her over seven miles away. Steve and I watched for Kristi. We never saw the RV get off at the exit, yet she said she was here.

"Oh no, she's getting off at the wrong exit!" Steve lamented, knowing we should be able to see her.

"Turn around," Kristi said, driving up behind us in a large pick-up.

"Where's the RV?" I asked, almost not wanting to hear the answer.

"They're just finishing up on it now. But I have a surprise for you both," she said excitedly.

She drove us in the pick-up back to Fred Ruth's dealership as they were finishing up on the RV. I offered to pay Fred's son who was working there that day. He would not accept a penny. As a matter of fact, he had another surprise for us as well. After thanking them repeatedly, Kristi drove the team about ten miles out into the desert to Fred's weekend home.

Fred wanted us to stay as his guests there. It was a ranch with horses, ponds, ducks, and other types of fowl. We hooked up to his barn right next to a grassy yard that was shaded with trees and was filled with exotic plants. We had not seen anything green in so long it was a feast for the eyes. What a glorious night!

Day 19—Friday, April 20

We woke up at 5:30 AM as Tex, the foreman, was feeding the horses. Tex was as country as they come and just as colorful in his words and actions. We had immediately fallen for the guy. We shared our adventures with him. In turn, he had several of his own to lay on us. He was a free spirit who had always done exactly what he wanted. He did not have much to show for it, but he was content with his life on the ranch. He was his own boss and life in the desert was very simple.

At 6:15, Steve drove the RV to a nearby restaurant to our start point. I went inside and bought our breakfast. After Steve inspected the RV, his bike, and the RowCycle, we were rowing by 7:10. We were going to have to climb from 2,700 to 4,500 feet over the next eight miles through Texas Canyon!

I cannot do justice to the grandeur of Texas Canyon. Rocks were stacked totem-pole style by nature. Large rocks were placed precariously on smaller ones below as erosion whittled away at the base. The climb through the canyon seemed easier because of the wondrous sights around us. We finally reached the peak and headed down a much gentler grade on the other side. We stopped for lunch after nineteen miles.

Kristi had parked the RV in the grass off the shoulder. After eating, Steve and I were ready to start again when I felt a jerk on the left wheel. I looked down only to find that I had broken an axle. I looked up the hill I had just come down at over twenty-five miles an hour. Had the axle broken while moving at that speed, it could have been serious. After Steve fixed this he found that he had two flat tires on his bike from sand burrs in the grass we were sitting on. I went ahead as Steve stayed behind to fix his tires.

We all met again in Wilcox. Kristi had arranged for us to meet with Debbie and Kathy, writers for the Wilcox and Benson papers. After the interview we climbed a gentle ten-mile grade. We finished outside of Bowie after going fifty-four miles. We drove to Bowie and found an RV park. I did my laundry while Kristi cooked our supper. We ate outside because Kristi was extremely ill, and the smell made her sick.

That evening, I called Wanice. Matters seemed to be falling apart at home. Jonathan missed me so much he cried daily and Jason was getting into trouble at school. They needed me at home. I deeply regretted that my children did not have their daddy. I went to sleep with negative thoughts and doubt that I was folllowing the right course. That night as I slept, I was haunted with an awful dream.

In the dream, I was asleep under a huge tree when it suddenly fell on me. However, the trunk was curved, and it fit right around me like a horseshoe. I could not get up, and I was suffocating. I was not seriously injured, but I was trapped under the heavy weight of the tree with no one around to help me.

I woke up and realized I was dreaming, but I felt as if the dream meant I would not be able to go forty miles the next day because of a disaster of some sort. As silly as the dream was, I had trouble going back to sleep. Finally at 3 AM I fell asleep but slept fitfully the rest of the night.

Day 20—Saturday, April 21

After rowing eighteen miles I was unusually tired, and the dream bothered me. I was so tired that I thought of stopping for the day. Kristi fixed a snack and an extra strong protein drink for me, and I had enough strength to begin rowing again. The next six miles were uphill. We climbed from 3,700 to 4,300 feet. At the base of the next large hill was a large, yellow sign. Kristi was standing there with my video camera. Finally, I could make it out: *Welcome to New Mexico, Land of Enchantment.*

We had made it across our second state. Steve and I gave each other a "high five" as we passed the sign and stopped for pictures. However, there was also another sign that said, "No bikes allowed." We examined our maps and saw that there were no alternate routes except for dirt roads, so after a break we started again. I felt funny about breaking the law, but I was not going to row on a dirt road.

Once again, we started up a hill. Soon after, a policeman passed, and he just waved at us and signaled with his lights as he passed by. I was incredibly tired as I continued up the hill. I began to hear that Voice in my heart again, "You can go another mile, can't you?" Then another, then another. After reaching what we thought was the top, Kristi informed us that it was not. My body was urgently calling for me to stop, but my heart was telling me everything was OK and to go, go, go! Words cannot describe the agony I was in. Steve had never seen me so tired. For the second time on the trip I rowed until I cried because the pain in my upper body was so intense. It was sheer torture.

We went another two miles up the hill before going over the top, only to be buffeted by a head wind. We felt it would blow from the east the rest of the day. We were at thirty-four miles. I began to believe for the first time that I was going to make it forty miles. At the bottom of the hill was a truck stop. Kristi was feeling weak, so we stopped there for a meal. This was the fourth day in a row she had been sick.

While eating and resting, I asked a trucker about the sign at the border that prohibited bikes on the interstate.

"That's just there so if you get run over, the police can say 'I told you so.' "

We all laughed before finishing rowing for the day. I had three or four miles of flat road. My odometer was at thirty-eight miles.

We were approaching Kristi when Steve turned and looked at me as if to say, *Are you going to tell her, or am I?* Steve knew me well enough to recognize that I would not be able to sleep if I went only thirty-eight miles, and it was physically possible to go forty. He told Kristi to go one more mile. Within twenty minutes we were passing her again, even though the head wind continued to blow against us. I looked down at my computer: thirty-nine miles. We were at the bottom of a small hill.

"Go one more mile," Steve instructed Kristi on the radio.

Understandably, Kristi was tired of moving the RV so she waited to see how far I could really go. The last mile was laboriously slow. I stopped several times on the little hill. I watched the computer count off the hundredths of a mile. Steve went ahead to the spot and pulled out his camera. Neither of us could believe it when my odometer finally read forty miles! We were spraying the "S" down when I realized that the name *Jesus* carried us across another state. Hallelujahs were in order.

Normally my actual rowing time was between six to eight hours. I looked at my watch. I had been rowing in an exhausted state against head winds, uphill, and with a spirit of discouragement for over nine tedious hours. This was the sixth straight day of rowing! As tough as the day was, I had seen nothing yet compared to what I was going to face in the days to come.

Fina, our gas sponsor, was not available in California or Arizona, so for the first time in New Mexico we filled up with Fina gas. I watched the gas meter turn and praised God that someone else was paying for it. Kristi drove to Deming to a motel, compliments of the Deming First Baptist Church. There was only one room. I slept in the RV to allow Kristi to be more comfortable.

6

The Storm—

Trusting in God, When Not in Control

Day 21—Sunday, April 22

I woke missing Wanice and the boys terribly. As I dressed for church, I noticed how much smaller my legs were when putting on my braces. As a matter of fact, my entire body was skinnier. Not wanting to wake Steve and Kristi, I went to breakfast by myself. While eating, I overheard a nearby conversation about the First Baptist Church of Deming, New Mexico. I walked over to the men and introduced myself. I learned that they were visiting evangelists named Nathan and Clark. Nathan Pillow somehow looked familiar. I knew his brother, Jerry, well. Both were ministers. We talked briefly before they left.

As I was leaving, I noticed a man having a hard time paying for his meal. A verse came to me "As you give, you will receive." As low on cash as I was, I did not want to ignore someone in need. What if God ignored me the next time I needed His help? I paid for his meal and then left as Steve and Kristi came in to eat.

I spoke during the Sunday School hour, followed by Nathan Pillow's message. I was so hungry for someone else's voice besides my own that I gobbled down every word he spoke. After the service I met the Harpers. As we would discover later, the only description for them was pure love. The Harpers invited us to stay with them when we rowed through Deming two days later.

Steve drove us to Las Cruces. We received directions to the church and arrived just in time. We were shuffling down the hall, and I was being introduced to the staff when I tripped. My face was just a foot from the floor as Steve's strong arms caught me. This was no small task since I outweighed Steve by fifty pounds. He helped me up as the rest of the staff breathed a sigh of relief.

I walked into the front of a well-appointed sanctuary onto a raised platform. After several preliminaries I proceeded to share my testimony. What occurred was an act of God. As I bared my heart, I could not see a dry eye. Heaven itself opened up, and I gave the invitation. Not a soul moved. I feel that God had done such a work that everyone simply sat there. After I finished, the pastor was speechless. He stood there trying to talk but couldn't. He closed the service with a prayer and asked everyone to buy a book. Between the books sold and the love offerings, most of that week's bills were paid. I thought back to early that morning and the bill I paid for the man in the restaurant. I wondered if he had been an angel. At any rate, I was thankful I had been obedient in a small way so God could bless us in a big way.

I kept Steve company as he drove us all the way back to Lordsburg while Kristi snoozed. On our way back to our start point for the next morning we stopped at a Fina station. While I lay there, Steve pumped the gas, washed the windows, bought me a soda pop, and checked our equipment. I couldn't believe what a servant he was. Within another hour we were back to Lordsburg. At midnight we pulled into the Shady Grove Truck Stop. There must have been 150 trucks there. Steve drove past rows of them before selecting a rather secluded spot. Steve and I were asleep by 12:30 with a full day of rowing only six hours away.

Day 22—Monday, April 23

Sometime during the early morning, Steve heard someone touching the outside of the RV. After looking around and not seeing anything, he went back to bed. At 6, we were up. Just as Steve was preparing to drive us to our start point, he saw a note taped to the RV's front window. It was from John Malone, a member of the church in Brawley, California. Out of all of the trucks in the yard, we had parked right beside his rig while he slept. He left $20 for us and a touching letter expressing his thanks that our paths had crossed again.

We started rowing at 7:30. It was another flat, boring day with a few small hills. The wind was from the south, then finally from the west.

All through the trip, Steve and I wanted to shoot a picture of the large whirlwinds filled with dust that blew by us from time to time, but we wanted a spectacular one.

When a whirlwind passed, we would comment, "Is that large enough? Nah! Not quite." This went on for days.

The wind was strong when something unusual happened. Suddenly Steve looked over his shoulder with an odd expression. *What's wrong?* I wondered. I started to look back when he said, "Look out!"

Just as I turned to look, a large sagebrush hit us from behind and rolled over us. It scratched both of us as it bounced from me to Steve. We watched it as it rolled off into the distance. Steve made the incident complete by remarking, "That was a close *brush* with death!" Steve and I loved corny jokes so we continued in that mood for an hour.

All morning we passed signs for a store that sold "authentic Indian jewelry." At eight miles an hour, you can read every word on every billboard. It became a hobby for us. There must have been twenty signs for this place. It was right at the Continental Divide. Steve and I became captivated with stopping to see this "authentic Indian jewelry." When we finally crossed the Continental Divide, there was the store. We were so excited. We rushed inside the store after Steve helped me into my chair, going immediately to the "authentic Indian jewelry."

I saw a cowboy kicking the floor and muttering curses. "Come here!" he yelled. I rolled over to him. He pulled a belt off of the wall and stuck it in my face. There in big, bold letters it said, "Made in Taiwan." Every belt on the wall read the same, "Made in Taiwan." I began laughing. Soon he was laughing, too. He had read all the same signs I had.

After a few more hills and plenty of flat desert we stopped at Exit 68 for the day. We had gone fifty-four miles.

We stopped at the First Baptist Church, Deming, to call the Harpers with whom we were to stay. Within a few minutes Mr. Harper led us to his home among exquisite mountains. The first thing I did was to take a genuine, honest-to-goodness bath. I looked in the mirror. I didn't recognize myself. I was lean, tan, and looked ten years older. After bathing, we fed his horses and followed the Harpers around the ranch.

Later, I watched another spectacular sunset with the mountains turning a reddish brown. I sat outside for an hour praying when I realized that the wind was picking up. It is always windy in the high desert, but this was becoming unusually strong. I noticed that something large was building on the horizon. I fell asleep wondering what it was.

Day 23—Tuesday, April 24

Mr. Harper woke us up at 6, and Mrs. Harper fixed us a hearty breakfast. The sunrise was beautiful, yet was somehow foreboding. We were rowing by 7:15 AM.

It was very windy from the west. That "something large" continued to build on the horizon. This was the strongest tail wind that we had experienced on the trip, so we didn't complain. Yet Steve and I kept a wary eye on the horizon behind us.

We passed through Deming, and Kristi did some shopping for the Harpers. Mr. Harper teased us playfully about how much we ate. We planned on having some fun with him that night.

At around 10 AM, we passed a man who was in bad shape and was all out of water and money. I gave him what change I had and gave him all my water. Soon after, at a break, my water was replenished and we moved on.

Suddenly Steve stopped by the side of the road and signaled for me to come see something. Crawling at a brisk pace along the side of the road was a copperhead snake. He appeared to be running from something. We watched him slither off into the desert before beginning again. We did not have long to find out what he was running from.

That particular day, Steve had a problem. He was out of clamps for my seat mechanism. They seemed to break about every third day, and this was the third day. He was thinking about his problem when he passed something on the road. It was a clamp. Steve could not believe it. But surely it was not the right size. Upon examining it, it was not only the right size, but brand new.

Steve also had another problem: the right rear light of the RV was burned out, and he needed a replacement. As he was riding along thinking about it, he passed something in the road. It was a light. Steve passed it by knowing that the chances of it being good and the right size were next to impossible. But then he thought about the clamp. He rode back, picked it up, and examined it. The filaments appeared to be intact. Even more incredible, it appeared to be the right size. At the next break he tried it. It worked!

Steve and I began looking on the ground for all our needs. This odd phenomenon would continue for the rest of Steve's stay on the trip in the form of wrenches, straps, change, or whatever Steve really needed. To be honest, I half expected to find manna.

I ate my lunch and later learned that I had eaten Kristi's also. That I had taken food from a pregnant woman would be the joke for the week. We finished the day at forty-one miles by 3 PM.

We drove back to Deming and ate with the Harpers again. After dinner, we brought in a large roast for Mr. Harper and flowers for Mrs. Harper. We kidded Mr. Harper about how much I ate and said we wanted to replenish his supply. He laughed but then was deeply moved that I would spend what little money we had on them. You would have thought we had bought him a fancy, imported sports car.

Later, I went out to feed the horses with Brother Harper. He commented that they appeared to be extremely nervous for some reason. I turned around, seeing something large from the corner of my eye. There, only a few hundred yards from us was a wall of sand thousands of feet high. It looked like someone had stood the desert on its side. I pushed my chair as quickly as possible toward the house. I wasn't scared. I wanted my camera. This was definitely the sand picture that we had been waiting for. After grabbing my camera and yelling for Steve and Kristi, it was upon us. The Harpers thought we were crazy as Steve, Kristi, and I stayed outside taking pictures of one another. The sand was so thick it was difficult for us to breathe. We made a dash for the house just as the worst of the storm hit. For the next two hours, the sand proceeded to blast everything in its path. It was followed by hail, rain, and thunder. We finally had our picture. But guess what? The camera battery was dead. The picture was overexposed. Mr. Harper told us that it was the worst sandstorm in the last fifty years.

That night both Mike Brantley and Greg Smith called me. They were two of my closest friends, and I badly needed to talk with them. They were full of encouragement and agreed I was doing the right thing. I was glad to hear from them also because I was down to sixty dollars and needed their words of faith in God for my success.

I looked into the sky filled with stars that were so thick it looked like a field of diamonds. It was funny. Moments ago the desert was trying to kill everything its path, yet now it shared its beauty. The desert was truly unpredictable. I could see the lights of Las Cruces over twenty-five miles away beyond the mountains to the east. I wished Wanice were there to share that moment with me.

Day 24—Wednesday, April 25

We finally had a day off. It was forty degrees outside. We ate breakfast in Deming with the Harpers at the Cactus Cafe. Afterwards, we drove to Las Cruces for Kristi's first medical appointment for her baby. The doctor told her that everything was normal but that she needed to gain more weight. I was praying that the trip would not be too hard on her. While she was at the doctor's, I cleaned the RV. This was not easy for me as I had to crawl on my hands and knees. Next, Steve and I washed away the sandstorm dirt off the bike and RowCycle. We bought a few bike parts, and then Steve cleaned the outside of the RV as I finished the inside. As tired as we were, we wanted to help Kristi.

My largest sponsor, DynCorp, had a great surprise waiting for us in Las Cruces. The Alamogordo division of DynCorp put us up that night at the Hilton.

We arrived at 4 PM and cleaned up. Kristi asked me if I would make all of the needed phone calls because she was very tired.

At 6:15, we drove thirty-five miles to the next church in Anthony. Part of the trip was down a dirt road which deposited dust all over our clean bike and RowCycle which meant that Steve would have to clean them all over again. We barely made it to the service at the Anthony Baptist Church. We found fifteen people waiting for us. Undaunted, I shared my testimony and sold two books. In the sight of God, no genuine church is "small." I was honored to share with them. We drove back to the Hilton and were all sleeping like babies in our plush surroundings.

Day 25—Thursday, April 26

We started rowing at 6:30, hoping to escape some of the desert heat later in the day. We began at 4,500 feet altitude and proceeded to row across twenty-three miles of flat, high desert. The early-morning temperature was a cool fifty. Soon after beginning, Steve and I realized that our water had turned sour. I spit it out of my mouth before telling Steve not to drink his. In the cool of the day, water was not a problem, and we went the first twenty miles without drinking. We replenished our supply at a break and were off again. Five miles later, we were moving over thirty miles an hour down a six-mile-long hill into Las Cruces. At the bottom, we checked the altimeter. It read 3,900 feet. We had lost 600 feet of altitude on a single hill!

We turned onto Highway 28 and for the first time since California and a few cities along the way, we were off the interstate. We began traveling down the secluded road when something occurred to Steve and me. We could hear birds singing in the trees. We saw children playing in yards. We suddenly realized how loud the interstate was and how much of rural America we had missed along the freeway. We feasted our eyes on plush pine trees and large pecan orchards that lined the highway. Other than Fred Ruth's paradise and Palm Springs this was the first green we had seen on the trip. The rowing seemed easier as my mind was filled with the wonders around us. I never thought that a bird singing could sound so sweet. We also realized how much pressure we were under on the interstate. We always had to have one eye in our rear-view mirror for trucks or someone needing the shoulder for an emergency.

As I rowed along the Voice in my heart said, "Don't worry about the money, Rob. If I take care of the lillies and birds of the field, how much more will I take care of you." I felt ashamed that I had worried so much about the money. I looked over at Steve. Here was a man who walked away from his job to be here. What a man of faith! I had no way knowing that during the next two weeks, almost all meals, lodging, and expenses were going to be paid for by churches, church members, and DynCorp. This was not only an answer to prayer for me but made Kristi's job of preparing meals considerably less. We would need the comfort God was giving us because one of the greatest physical challenges of the trip lay ahead.

At lunch, Kristi and I began talking about the doctor's appointment and about her need to gain weight. During the course of the discussion she asked if she could have a few weeks off of the trip as we passed through Texas. I made it an even month, feeling that the rest would do her good. I felt that the last part of the trip would be extremely difficult for all of us, and I wanted her to rest as much as possible before she returned. We finished the day at forty-five miles, halfway between Las Cruces and El Paso. We drove back to the Hilton and stayed one more night courtesy of DynCorp.

Day 26—Friday, April 27

We said "ta ta" to the Hilton and were rowing by 7:45. We passed through several small towns along Hwy 28 before slowly moving back out into the desert. ABC, Channel 7, came out from Las Cruces and videotaped. It would be seen over most of New Mexico several times over the course of the next few days.

Kristi stayed behind to take a nap. Steve and I moved ahead to the Texas border. The roads changed numbers at the border. We also took a different route into El Paso because the road we had decided to travel was reduced to a very small road with no shoulder. Steve put arrows down on two of our turns for Kristi, but when we came to the third, he decided to wait for Kristi before proceeding. I filled my water container from Steve's supply and went on ahead. Now all three of us were at different locations. I prayed that God would protect and guide us until we rejoined again. I also prayed that the RowCycle would not break down. Without Steve with me, I was trapped in the RowCycle if I had a problem. We were in the El Paso city limits when I came to the corner of I-10 and Mesa. I radioed Steve that I was getting on I-10 because Mesa appeared to go over a large mountain to the left of the pass (El Paso means "The Pass").

Steve told me that he was going to wait there and inform Kristi where I was when she caught up. I crept along the busy highway at the rate of four miles an hour because of the angle of ascent. Within forty-five minutes, Kristi finally passed me. I was out of water, so I instructed her to exit at the next off-ramp. Steve soon caught up with me and gave me water. We had our socks scared right off by the traffic as I-10 narrowed to make its way through "the pass." Cars passed within a few feet of us at over sixty miles an hour. After twenty minutes of this, we found the next exit and caught up with Kristi.

During lunch we talked about finally being in Texas. We became so excited until I realized something.

"We have gone over 700 miles! That's great, but you know what? We have another 700 miles of Texas to cross before making it to Fort Worth. Not only that, but we have 972 miles of Texas total to cross!" We could have spelled "Jesus Christ, King of Kings and Lord of Lords"!

I was so exhausted after climbing the last big hill and with the realization of our present location, I was forced to ask, "Whose turn is it in the RowCycle?" There were no volunteers!

We started again. Turning left at Mesa Boulevard, we intersected with Montana (Highway 180) and headed east. We later found that if we had stayed on Mesa, we would have crossed Montana. But we would have missed testing our lobotomy effectiveness.

Just two blocks down Montana we passed the First Baptist Church, El Paso, where we were to speak the following Sunday. Kristi stopped, let them know we were alive and kicking, and used their phone to make her daily calls.

After another ten miles we finished for the day at forty-five miles. We looked east and saw the next mountain range we would need to cross— the Hueco (Waco) Mountains. We marveled at their size. We didn't know that just beyond the mountains lay the real challenge. We drove to the house of Larry and Dorothy Jones. Larry and I would find that we had a lot in common.

A tall man with a limp walked out to greet us. He invited us in and within minutes we were at home. We talked for hours. I learned that Larry wore a prosthesis. He had lost his leg in Vietnam. We talked and compared the physical pain that we felt as the result of nerve damage— mine in my back and his in his leg. It was the same type of pain.

"It is like sticking your toe into a wall socket," he said. We talked about how we dealt with the pain that we would have for the rest of our lives. We both agreed that the best way to handle it was to not think about it, pick up the pieces, and go on with our lives.

Later, we went to sleep in comfortable beds. "Sleep, it is a gentle thing, beloved from pole to pole," wrote Will Shakespeare. How absolutely true! The storm was behind us, but a far greater challenge was ahead.

7

El Capitan—
We Wrestle Not Against Flesh and Blood

Day 27—Saturday, April 28

After Dorothy fixed a large breakfast for us, we were on the road by 7:30 AM. Kristi received word that a friend had sold a piece of property and was going to give part of the profits to them. This came just in time to make their house payments. God had met their first month's bills.

Meanwhile, Steve and I were having our own problems. We were beginning to climb the Hueco Mountains. The first mountain was nine miles long. I was having to stop every half mile for a break. Saturdays were always the hardest because it was the fifth or sixth consecutive day for me to row. As soon as I cleared the top of the first mountain, I was excited until I saw that it was merely the first of many. Each time when I thought I was through, there was another mountain. As a matter of fact I would have to climb seven mountains in a row.

That's when that little Voice in my heart spoke again, "In life, there's always one more hill. It's a lie to say that, 'I'm on a financially difficult hill, so God will surely understand if I don't tithe now.' Or say that, 'I'm on a work-related hill, so surely God will understand if I don't spend time with my family right now.' Or even say that, 'I'm on a lazy hill, so surely God will understand if I don't work right now.' Being on a hill is never an excuse for being weak. I have given you the tools with which to work and get over the hill. You tell all those churches out there to begin pulling on the handles and trust Me. I'll get them over the hill." From that moment on I would close the service with that statement right before the invitation that God had already given me.

At the top of the mountain range we passed through a border patrol.

I'm sure he thought he had seen it all when the next vehicle through his gate was a RowCycle. He waved me on with a curious look. I told him that an RV was with me. Kristi told me later that he just waved her through as well. The next twenty-one miles were tough, rolling hills. After thirty-eight miles, we paused for lunch, and then averaged over twelve MPH over the level plains the rest of the day. We were abetted by a terrific tail wind with a terrific tail wind. Along the way we saw seven deer eating the sparsely placed desert grass. This lofty plain received barely enough water for dry, plain grass to grow.

After fifty miles we were about to stop for the day when I had a nagging feeling that we needed to go on. That was the smartest decision I could have made considering what was going to happen two days later. We started again with the wind so strong that it actually pushed Steve uphill. Steve's maximum speed was forty-seven miles per hour. Mine was thirty-five. We covered another ten miles in less than an hour.

We headed back to the Jones Residence in El Paso at 4 PM after a sixty-mile rowing day. We all went to Juarez, Mexico, together. From El Paso, Juarez completely fills the horizon. It is awesome, a city of over a million people. I bought gifts for the entire family for only $10. We were impressed with the extreme poverty that filled the streets and faces of the people we met. Beggars were everywhere. I think I know how Jesus must have felt when He was surrounded by multitudes of the poor, sick, and dying.

After returning to El Paso, we ate at a Mexican restaurant. However, Kristi was too sick to hold it down. We felt sorry for her.

I told Larry and Dorothy about my difficulty in climbing the Hueco Mountains. Larry looked at Dorothy wondering if he should break some bad news to me. He proceeded, thinking that I should know the truth.

"Rob, the hills you just climbed are nothing compared to El Capitan. It is one of the steepest grades in New Mexico, with some of the worst cross winds in America."

I couldn't believe it. How could it be worse than the Hueco Mountains? I did not have long to wait to see the truth for myself.

Day 28—Sunday, April 29

Dorothy ironed my shirts and fixed breakfast. Having freshly ironed shirts for the first time on the trip spoiled me. I would iron all my own shirts until Wanice arrived to do them.

I spoke to the youth at First Baptist Church, El Paso. After that, we ate lunch with the Joneses and said our good-byes. Steve drove us to Las Cruces to Calvary Baptist Church. We changed clothes at the Hampton Inn compliments of Calvary and then went to the service. We met with Sam, the pastor, and prayed.

This was going to be the first time I would use both the "always-one-more-hill" illustration and close with *JESUS* as an acronym. However, because I was having difficulty with a brace and there was no podium, I spoke while sitting. Nevertheless, the Spirit moved both the congregation and me.

Steve and I returned to the motel at 11:30. Thank goodness the following day was a day off. We were exhausted.

Day 29—Monday, April 30

Steve drove while I cleaned the RV and ironed my shirts. We were going to Alamogordo Air Force Base where I was to speak with the employees of the DynCorp installation there.

We drove over the steepest grade in New Mexico with a breathtaking view of the valley below. We arrived at the base gate at 12:30. After signing us in, we went to the PX (Post Exchange) so I could have my thick, unruly hair cut. My editor and others always teased me because my hair was down over my eyes like many teenagers wear theirs.

Upon leaving the PX a bizarre thing happened. We were going across the parking lot when a car began honking at us. We went faster, thinking we were blocking the way. The car continued to honk its horn as if to hurry us up. This irritated me so I stopped and turned to face this seemingly insensitive person. I was staring right at my wife's Aunt Eleanor. She smiled as my face betrayed my anger and slowly changed to a look of recognition. She and her husband, retired Brigadier General Cecil Jenkins, had driven clear from San Antonio to hear me address the personnel there. I was overwhelmed that they would drive so far.

I met Jack, the DynCorp personnel manager, and then was taken to the gate for an official police escort onto the base. The police car blocked traffic as I rowed across the base to a hangar. I addressed the men there and met the wing commander as well. I was given money for paralysis research as well as several beautiful plaques. I even sat in a T-38 fighter plane for publicity shots. Afterwards we went to the officers' club for a reception, and I addressed the men there. I spoke through tears as I looked at my uncle, the general whom I respected greatly. We ate a huge meal. Jack gave us the leftovers which we would be eating for over a week. Still hungry, we ate again with Cecil and Eleanor at the officers' club. Steve drove us back 150 miles to our starting point. I kept Steve company and put all the food away while Kristi rested. I was excited about the ordeal that awaited me there. The words *El Capitan* challenged me. If Larry Jones was right, one of the most monstrous challenges of the trip was lying in wait waiting for me.

We arrived at 11:30 PM and parked on the side of the road beside our start point. We went to sleep at 1 AM. The wind blew against the RV all night and even shook it from time to time. The wind did not bother me because it would be a tail wind and would actually cut my work in half.

Day 30—Tuesday, May 1

Matters were going to start off bad and worsen. Steve greeted me at the door with a sick look on his face. "What's wrong?" I asked.

He didn't say a mumbling word. He pointed to the tree that stood beside the RV. It was bent over with the wind. I looked at it with a horrified expression. It was bending the wrong way!

I got into the RowCycle as a terrific head wind proceeded to blow sand and dust into our faces. It was steady at twenty miles an hour with gusts over forty. We started at 7:45 AM. I was about to tested. How badly did I want to succeed? I rowed minute after minute and hour after hour into a terrific head wind that was getting stronger. I had no momentum. The average stroke was around 100 pounds on level ground. Uphill was so difficult that I grunted with every stroke. Sand and dust filled the air. Steve and I did not talk. We was going to have to outlast the elements. I became light headed as the pain grew so intense in my arms, hands, back and stomach I thought I would pass out.

"Stop, Steve!" I cried. "I can't take any more!" Beaten men, we both crawled into the RV after six hours of effort that covered only eighteen miles. After lunch we all took a two-hour nap. I was incredibly tired as I climbed back into the RowCycle. We tried drafting behind the RV, but the wind was so strong that if we got even three feet away from the vehicle, it would whip around the side and stop us in our tracks. I was worn-out and beat down when at 4 PM, I yelled that I had gone the limit. I looked at my odometer. After ten hours of rowing, it read only twenty miles. I was badly discouraged and frazzled, but I knew I had given it my best shot, so I was not disappointed in myself. We drove to a nearby town for supplies, and I had to call Wanice. I needed to draw from her strength. I longed to hear my boys say one more time, "You can do it, Dad."

We drove to an old abandoned restaurant to use the phone. After talking with my family and being somewhat encouraged, a funny thing happened. I guess God knew that the moment was too heavy, and we all needed a laugh. I needed to use the bathroom, and it was far too difficult for me to avail myself of the RV, so I went around the corner out of sight. Steve and Kristi were inside talking. Steve looked around to see if I were OK and make sure the wind had not blown me to the Land of Oz. He was shocked to see an empty phone booth.

He went into "GI Joe" mode. Something was wrong with his older brother. Steve was coming to the rescue. He grabbed a weapon and approached the building like a Stealth Bomber. He peered inside to see the would-be attackers. Not finding them, he moved with catlike reflexes around the perimeter of the building as we had been taught in the service. He peered around the corner to take on the enemy and crush the onslaught of their attack. We need not go into what he saw, but he returned to the RV somewhat disappointed that he did not have to test his military prowess.

We returned to a nearby rest area and ate supper. I read three books of the Bible seeking comfort for my discouragement. I asked God to change the weather several times before falling into deep sleep due to total exhaustion. I woke several times during the night as the wind shook the RV like a rag doll.

Day 31—Wednesday, May 2

"Boom!" went the thunder jolting me out of my sleep. Over and over, lightning lit up the inside of the RV like midday. "Wham!" went the wind as it threw debris against the side of the RV. I lay there not wanting to look outside. After brief periods of sleep, the sun finally started to light up the horizon.

The morning of May 2, I was sore and tired from the day before (par for the course, of course), and my hands ached and throbbed. I watched as Kristi gently rubbed my hands and thought how tough it was for her. Here she was, pregnant, but still here to help me. But my hands were so sore to the touch that she stopped rubbing. I could not even close my hands in a fist. I was in trouble and was painfully aware of it! As I looked around, I could not believe what I saw. God had answered our prayer for changing the weather. The head wind now blew from between forty to sixty miles per hour. The temperature dropped to thirty-eight, and it rained. Conditions were so bad we wore extra clothing, gloves, and heavy rain suits. I was absolutely miserable sitting out there.

Just before leaving, we said our daily prayer for strength and courage. After praying, we began rowing east toward the dark ominous object ahead: El Capitan. It was throwing everything it had at us. Who would have the final victory was yet to be seen. The head winds bore down on us with a vengeance. Clouds covered the horizon and met the desert in all four directions. Steve and I were averaging three miles per hour as the wind beat us back. At 9 AM, we stopped at a rest area. I sat outside in the cold and ate a snack that Steve brought out. We started rowing again. The gusts of wind were getting stronger. The cold caused arthritic-like pains in my hands. Somehow cold water was leaking through my rain suit and dripping down my sweaty back. Conditions were unbearable for our fingers as we had to fix a broken seat clamp on the RowCycle.

We began our ascent of El Capitan when I saw something in my mind's eye. It was the demon that Dave had described standing in the middle of the road. He was pushing against the RowCycle and laughing at my feeble attempt to fight his size and power. I began to pray for the angels that Dave had seen, and I persisted beyond all human barriers. I had no strength left, but I continued somehow. I wondered if the angels were grunting as loud as I was. Slowly the tenths of a mile crept by and we stopped for lunch at a rest area. I was too tired to get into the RV. Besides, if I got out of my wet clothes into the dry RV, I probably would not be able to start again. Kristi fixed four plates of food and I ate outside.

I started again. Steve caught up with me later. The head winds were now so fierce it was impossible to hear each other speak.

Just then a pick-up pulled up behind us. A cowboy jumped out. "What in the world are you doing?" he asked, looking at us as if we were crazy.

"I'm rowing across America," I said, realizing how crazy it sounded. He gazed at both of us and then at the weather. He was sure he had run into two loonies.

"Hey, throw your stuff in the back of my truck, and I'll take you to the top. You don't know what you guys are in for up ahead. I hate driving up this mountain in a truck."

I explained that this was a Guinness World Record and that we could not cheat by even one inch. After attempting one more time to convince us to join him, he climbed into his warm truck and drove away, shaking his head and throwing a "God bless you" our way.

We rounded the corner and saw what I thought was a wall. It was not. It was the road!

Then we spotted a sign. We could not quite make it out. It looked like it had been in a war zone. The sides were bent and paint was peeling off. It was actually shaking worse then we were. As we approached the sign foot by foot up the steep grade against the wind, we could finally make it out. It declared: *Dangerous Crosswinds.*

Steve and I glanced at each other and thought together: *No kidding!*

However, we did not know that the mountain on the right side of the road was protecting us against those crosswinds. Just after passing the sign, we were hit by winds of up to one hundred miles an hour. It was blowing poor Steve all over the road. I was much more stable, but I had to correct my direction with each stroke. Between the wet road and hurricane-force winds, it blew Steve dangerously close to the road and passing motorists. Somehow, after half a mile of unbridled fury, we moved past that gap in the mountains, and the hurricane-force winds were dissipated a little. But we were nearing the top, and the head winds increased their attack, seemingly trying to stop us. The wind almost took on the quality of a living creature. It was the enemy!

Finally we stopped at 2:00 for the day. The mountain had won for the day. I looked at my odometer. In seven hours of torment, I had covered only twelve miles. As a matter of fact, in just two days we had lost 47.2 miles. But I looked up at El Capitan and vowed that I would return. The words I had spoken to every church came to my lips, "If God is for us, there is no power that can stop us."

I crawled into the RV. It was spotless. Kristi had cleaned it from front to back. She had driven sixty miles to Carlsbad while we slept. I picked up supplies there while Kristi bought a maternity dress. We drove to the house of Chuck and Mildred Crane for dinner and then spoke to a Baptist church in Carlsbad. I followed through, even though I was about to drop.

Steve drove us back to our start point for the following morning. It was already dark, and El Capitan stood there waiting for the contest to resume. The howling winds continued. We had been told that eighteen-wheelers had been blown over as they crossed El Capitan. We prayed that we would not be added to that statistic. We all slept with one eye open as the wind sardonically laughed at us.

Day 32—Thursday, May 3

I believe in miracles and feel that one occurred overnight: the storm broke. The winds were back to a mere twenty-five miles per hour. The demon was gone. I was rowing by 7:15 as a spectacular sunrise greeted us. The clouds were leaving. Steve and I had only one mile before we reached the top. Within twenty minutes, we were there. We had won! And to the victor went a breathtaking view of Texas and New Mexico. We stopped and snapped pictures of the highest point we would go on the entire trip. I read the elevation sign over and over: *5,695 Feet.*

As I passed El Capitan, it seemed so peaceful. It wasn't the same mountain as the day before. We had won this time, and I continued to make bold statements about God at churches. I knew that the enemy would return.

We descended the other side of the mountain in just a few hours. Once at the base, we had to cross small roller-coaster-style hills as we kept going toward Carlsbad, New Mexico.

We stopped at Carlsbad Caverns for lunch after thirty-six miles. I could not get enough to eat. I finally stopped eating due to my fatigue, not being full. Then we entered into Carlsbad Caverns and saw the largest cavern in the world. We had to descend 700 feet below the surface by elevator. Once inside, we walked for two miles and looked at the wonders below. I pushed my chair most of the way and propelled myself through some narrow passages with Steve and Kristi's help.

Once back on the hot surface above, we began again. After twenty-one more miles of head winds and hills, I rowed into Carlsbad to Chuck and Mildred Cranes's driveway. We had covered a daily total of fifty-seven miles! En route, a few reporters interviewed us. That night Mildred fixed a huge meal. Along with gorging myself, I drank tea, coffee, and a soft drink. I would pay for that later in the night. You know what I mean? After dinner I weighed myself for the first time on a scale that was accessible to me. I stood there gawking at the scale. I had lost seventeen pounds! I had gone through only three states. Would I make it?

Then I called Wanice. The sound of her sweet Texas accent buoyed my whole being. I wanted to see her so much. She was being so selfless about all this. Wanice had arranged all four weeks of replacements for Kristi. My family and friends were on the way to the rescue. It reminded me of the cavalry in a movie. Then the team sacked out early. But you guessed it. Caffeine was coursing through my system. I listened as the clocks ticked and chimed the hours away. The final chime I heard was three. At last I faded off to sleep.

8

The Home Stretch—
One Goal at a Time

Day 33—Friday, May 4

The alarm went off three hours after I had fallen asleep. We rowed away from the Cranes around 8. Kristi was becoming sicker and sicker and did not eat.

We turned down Mesa to Green Street and went Highway 180. Once again we had a ten- to twenty-five-mile-per-hour head wind! *When is it going to turn around?* I wondered. We were able to go thirty-one miles by lunch and stopped at the Halfway Cafe (halfway between Carlsbad and Hobbs). I was rowing again by 2 PM when a truck pulled up behind us. The man introduced himself as Jim Burrows.

"I'm the chairman of deacons from Taylor Memorial Baptist Church in Hobbs. You'll be coming to our church next week. We have a special surprise waiting for you."

The standing joke for the day was, "It's flat between Carlsbad and Hobbs." We had heard that several times. Obviously these people do not use altimeters. Although the terrain looked smooth, Hobbs was 500 feet higher than Carlsbad. In a RowCycle this is a significant difference! Several times Steve and I commented when struggling uphill, "This hill is just a mirage. Everybody knows that it's flat between Carlsbad and Hobbs."

Kristi needed a nap, so she pulled over seven miles ahead. I was traveling seven miles per hour, so this meant an hour of rowing. But the wind began to pick up and soon with six miles to go, I was traveling only six miles per hour. The wind picked up in velocity again. With five miles to go, I was now down to five miles per hour. I was two miles closer, but the bottom line was—I was still an hour from the RV. The wind became frenzied, and with with four miles to go, I was crawling along at four miles MPH and then three. It took almost two hours for us to travel the last seven miles.

We were bushed when arriving at the RV. Among her duties she had written out a list of responsibilities for her replacements.

We drove to a nearby oil field and parked for the night. It was peaceful, the only sounds being the methodical creaking of a nearby oil well as the head moved up and down and an occasional "moo" from the cows in the field. We walked around a bit. The oil field sent good and bad memories rushing from the past. Yet, even the good memories reminded me that I had been able-bodied until working in an oil field. Steve and Kristi took a long, romantic walk, and we were all asleep by 8:30 PM.

Day 34—Saturday, May 5

I awoke with an all-too-familiar pain in my lower back. I had a bladder and kidney infection! I knew I needed to start taking an antibiotic quickly before I grew sick. Had I caught it soon enough? Only time would tell. Being a paraplegic, I could not feel that area of my body until infection was so severe that an able-bodied person would be doubled over with pain. I prayed with an intensity I had seldom experienced. A bad infection could result in fever, loss of strength, and severe sickness. My goal was to row to my home in Fort Worth. I was not going to concern myself about the rest of the trip until later.

We began rowing at 7 AM. We could not believe it! The winds were out of the east again!

The enemy was about to strike, as he had throughout. We rowed through Hobbs while Kristi stayed behind for a nap. We had already passed Hobbs by the time Kristi caught up and called the press. It was too late; the media did not have time to respond. Kristi had also called home. Steve and Kristi had allowed some folks to stay there free of charge as a favor. The way they repaid Steve and Kristi for their kindness was to break furniture and leave filth everywhere. Kristi asked them to leave before she returned home. The full extent of the damage would not be discovered until Kristi arrived later that week. The enemy was attacking them severely.

After twenty-six miles of fighting the wind, we called it a day at the Texas border. We had entered Texas for the second and final time. I felt dead and hurt from six days of head winds and my fight with El Capitan. We sprayed the "S" on the road and realized that the name *Jesus* had just gotten us across our third state. Three down and ten to go!

Steve drove back two-and-a-half hours to Roswell, New Mexico. Along the way, I did the bookkeeping and realized that almost all meals and lodging for the past two weeks had been provided by churches and DynCorp.

Day 35—Sunday, May 6

I spoke at a Southern Baptist Church in Roswell. There had been a tragic air-show accident the day before in the area, so spirits were low. God spoke through me and helped in their despair. After the service a woman cried and hugged me. I learned later that her husband had died from falling off an oil derrick—similar to my own accident. While signing books, a young man in uniform approached me.

"Rob, I don't have any money, but I do have something I want to give you." He reached down and pulled two medals off of his chest.

"These are for courage and honor. Please accept these from me with the utmost respect." He saluted me and walked away. I wore these with great honor on my helmet strap for the rest of the trip. He would never know how much a lift he had given me.

We ate a steak dinner with Brother Lamar, the associate pastor, and then drove to Hobbs where we stayed at the Hobbs Motor Inn compliments of Taylor Memorial Baptist Church.

We had a brief team meeting in my room. Almost breathlessly I asked the team, "I need you to take some responsibilities from me. I am growing weaker by the day due to the infection and exhaustion. I barely have enough strength to row and speak." I had done my own washing and ironing since the fifth day of the trip. Kristi agreed to take over those duties.

After the meeting, Steve worked on the RowCycle, fixed our protein drinks, cleaned the RV, then carried our stuff into the motel.

Later, at Taylor Memorial, I met with Brother Dale, the associate pastor, and then Dean Mathis, the pastor. Doug Cosby, retired tight end with the Dallas Cowboys, shared his testimony. Then I delivered mine. The church took up a love offering for us and at the close of the service, we were both mobbed. Doug was signing autographs while I signed books. We were about thirty feet apart as we tried to make our way toward each other. He would sign an autograph and then take one step toward me. I would sign one book and then take a step with my braces and crutches towards him. Finally, we made it to each other and spoke for a minute. I was honored to meet such a Christian sports hero.

Day 36—Monday, May 7

Glory! The wind was finally out of the west. As we began rowing we were greeted by Larry, Kathy, and Cody (members of Taylor Memorial) at the start point. Kathy mentioned that she couldn't sleep so she had prayed for me all night. She didn't know exactly why sleep eluded her. I did. She was a prayer warrior who had helped pray my infection away or at least into remission.

After thirty-two miles, the local media interviewed us as we stopped for lunch. At long last, we were moving out of the worst part of the desert. The West Texas fields seemed to go forever. The flat, freshly plowed fields would disappear into the horizon in every direction. We viewed the typical West Texas home—cotton fields in the front yard and an oil well in the back.

After a few hills, but with the wind at our backs, we finished for the day at forty-five miles. We grabbed a two-hour nap under massive oak trees near the stop point. Steve cooked supper while I divided up vitamins in packets for the following week. My hands hurt so badly it was difficult to handle the little pills, but I prepared a month's supply.

Steve couldn't find my water bottle to fix our water for the next day. Since Kristi was resting, he didn't want to wake her up by moving the RV, so he rode his bike all the way back to our stop point. While I waited for Steve's return I watched another of God's masterpiece sunsets. I thought of Wanice, Jason, and Jonathan while I looked at the moon. I wondered what they were doing at that instant. I hoped that Wanice was looking at the moon from the other side of Texas and was thinking of me.

After it was completely dark, I sat there helplessly looking down a pitch-black road. I nervously waited for Steve. *Had anything happened? What was taking him so long?* I strained my eyes to see anything when suddenly I saw a green light floating along a few feet from the ground. What was this, a UFO attack? As it came closer it pulled off of the road and toward the RV. After another hundred feet I could make out Steve's profile on his bike. The green light was a phosphorous light stick he used to light his way.

"What took you so long?" I asked.

"The water bottle had blown quite a ways away before I found it. Then I took my time getting back in the darkness. I couldn't find the edge of the road."

After the adventure, Steve cleaned the kitchen, and we fell asleep.

Day 37—Tuesday, May 8

Rowing by 8, we went twenty miles to Lamesa on semi-flat ground. Kristi drove ahead eight miles to nap and fix lunch. With the wind at our backs, we arrived too early for lunch, so we moved on ahead. Steve and I were out of radio range when Kristi tried to start the RV. It would not start! Kristi began walking for help, then returned to the RV. Two men in a truck stopped to help her a few minutes later. There are a few good men left!

As Steve and I stopped for a snack, we wondered where Kristi was. Ten miles east of Lamesa, we descended from the "Cap Rock" (the drop from the high West Texas plains to lower Central Texas). We paused at the top from our lofty perch and looked east. We felt almost like Moses on Mount Nebo gazing over into the Promised Land. There was lush greenery ahead. We were finally out of the high desert. We came to a three-mile-long hill. Before reaching the bottom, I was moving at thirty-two MPH. I slowed down to fifteen when I felt a hard jerk to the right. Losing control for a split second, I slowed to a stop. My right axle had broken. Once again, the timing was miraculous. If it had broken while moving at that clip, the crash would have been gut-wrenching.

Steve and I had a little water left, but we were extremely hungry. Where was Kristi? After an hour-long wait, we saw her coming down off Cap Rock. Those two men were following her to make sure she was OK. They explained what was wrong with the RV. It was loose wiring to the ignition. We were thankful that Kristi was OK. I stopped rowing for the day at 3 because of the broken axle. We drove two hours to Odessa for a speaking engagement at Crescent Park Baptist Church the following day.

Day 38—Wednesday, May 9

As Steve and Kristi ate breakfast in their room in the motel, I went to the dining room where a revelation awaited me. I sat there reading my daily Scriptures when I suddenly envisioned the first seven chapters of this book. I quickly wrote down a synopsis, along with general ideas for the book's contents.

We fixed the axle and changed tubes three times because the tire was also defective. We then headed to the service at Crescent Park.

The Odessa newspaper came to the church. We ate a fellowship meal, and then I spoke at the 6:30 PM service. Guess what I forgot again?—my Bible! If you learn nothing else from my odyssey, it is this: hang onto your Bible! Put it in a back pack or roll it in a wheelbarrow, if it's a king-size volume!

Steve drove us back from Odessa to Lamesa. We arrived at 10:30 PM and stayed on the side of the road in a church parking lot. We were asleep by midnight after Steve and I made our protein and performance drinks for the next day.

The temperature dropped to forty-five during the night.

Day 39—Thursday, May 10

Kristi was extremely sick, and we were becoming ore distressed by the minute. Ron Jenkins, a reporter with the Fort Worth *Star-Telegram*, met us and made several pictures. He had driven all the way from Fort Worth to see us and to cover a few other stories to justify the trip. He brought doughnuts which we couldn't eat until later (Steve and I did not eat sugar during the day because of the bad effect it has on endurance).

I started rowing by 8:30 AM. We had ten- to-twenty-mile-per-hour wind out of the east again! You are all too aware of what those winds did to our time. One highlight of the day: the scenery was becoming greener by the minute. I thought of an old hymn: "In shady green pastures so rich and so sweet, God leads His dear children along." And He was doing exactly that!

Several people along the way were fortunate enough to see our cattle-and-horse roundup techniques. This was indeed a strange phenomenon, but it happened several times a day throughout the West Texas plains. When Steve and I would pass livestock on the side of the road, they would stop and stare at us. I'm relatively sure they had never seen a RowCycle before, pumping along with an American flag flying over it. Once we had their attention, Steve would make a cattle call that sounded like a bull who had not encountered a cow for years. Then I would follow up with a bass "moo." What happened next was the peculiar part. Cattle would sometimes follow us for miles, at least as long as the fences permitted. Ron did not believe we could do this until he saw it for himself. After twenty-six miles, we ate lunch at 12:30. We began again at 1:30. I finished at 4:30 with only forty miles for the day. Then it was on to Snyder.

Day 40—Friday, May 11

We were prepared to begin rowing by 7:30 in the morning when a man walked up and asked about the letter on the road that we had spray painted in front of his house. I thought we were in trouble for defacing public property. He suddenly yelled over his shoulder to another fellow who was working on a tractor in the field behind him.

"I told you this was them. This is the guy we read about. Boy, I hope that the rain doesn't wash this letter away. He really stopped right here."

We talked for a moment before beginning. The rest of the morning was more of flat West Texas. The wind was out of the south, though. For the first time in days, we did not have a head wind. The terrain was turning greener as we approached North Central Texas which had been a flood area only a week before. For the first time since the trip began, we began to run into humidity. We were not used to it, and it was a little hard to breath the humid air.

After lunch in Roby, a dog began following us. He was a cute rascal, so at first we didn't mind, but after a few miles of his presence and after a few close calls with cars, we tried to run him off. Nothing worked. We yelled, Steve even chased him. He finally became bored and tired with this routine.

We finished at 4 after forty-seven miles. We drove back into Roby and stayed at an RV park by Cottonwood Creek. Kristi was very sick and could not cook, so she heated up a can of beans for us and went to bed. I ate two bowls of beans, but I was still incredibly hungry. I was going to call Wanice. Since Kristi was in bed, we could not move the RV. I was prepared to push my wheelchair to town when I met the park owner, Mr. Terry, who offered to take me there. Upon my return I watched television in the park recreation room and took a nap. I was trying to ignore the hunger that was growing by the minute. I was burning 6,000 calories per day, and a couple of bowls of beans were hardly an appetizer. I went back to the RV after dark and took a bath with Steve's help. I told Steve I could not wait another minute for food. He heated up two large cans of stew for me before cleaning up the kitchen and going to bed. With a full stomach, I slept fairly well. I dreamed of seeing my family at our stop point the next day.

Day 41—Saturday, May 12

I was rowing by 7:30 AM. The day had finally arrived. We descended from 2,000 to 1,200 feet, going down several humongous hills. A few were so steep they were totally exposed to the surroundings. They contained dangerous grades and wind currents. We went forty-two miles by lunch and took a nap. We began again at 1:45 in Albany, a gracious town with the traditional town hall with large clocks.

Steve and I stopped in at a barber shop to call the local press. We met the owner, Dave, standing outside his shop. Every once in a while he would glance down, smile, and then continue talking. After doing this for the third time, I looked down to see what he was staring at. To my horror, he was standing on a gravestone. Why would he have such a gratified look while bordering on the macabre? Good grief, his name was on the stone! I could not resist asking, "Dave, why are you standing on your gravestone, and why is it here?"

"Almost everybody asks me that," he responded. "I have two answers. Number one—I'm ready to go. Number two—when my father died, the kids were strapped with all of the expense and details of the funeral. Not me! I'm paid for. They can just drop me in a hole and set this on top. I'm not going to be there, anyway." There is plenty of spiritual thought there. Dave was ready. Are you?

Kristi caught up and we were off again. The RowCycle broke but

Steve, as always, had it fixed in minutes. We went from Albany almost to Breckenridge. We passed a sign soon after. It said "Fort Worth—117 Miles." I turned to Steve and said, "I can spit that far."

We went sixty-two miles for the day. We waited for Wanice until 6 PM at a prearranged location. I looked east and waited for over an hour for my wife and boys, but didn't show up. I was so disappointed. Steve drove us over to Colorado City to the next church. I hoped to meet Wanice there. We arrived at church, but no Wanice. We were not sure what to do next when a car pulled up. It was the pastor.

"There is someone at my house who is kind of anxious to see you," he reported with a smile. He led us to his house only two miles away, but to me it was like 2,000. He seemed to be driving so slowly. Finally we reached it. He walked inside. Approximately one second later, two comets zipped through the door and across the yard. Within seconds my two boys were in my lap with hugs that could have put a grizzly bear to shame. We could not let go of each other. Then from the door of the RV came Wanice—to me the sweetest woman on earth. She walked over and kissed me. We looked into each other's eyes, exchanging six weeks of lost affection in an instant.

Wanice was shocked at my weight loss. We drove to a hotel, compliments of the church. Wanice, the boys, and I slept in the RV and let Steve and Kristi sleep in the motel.

Day 42—Sunday, May 13

The cavalry had arrived in West Texas! For the next month, Kristi would be able to rest. Our friends and family would go with us for the next 800 miles. Wanice rose early and, with a fresh burst of energy, cleaned the RV. I was reminded what a hard worker she was. Wanice also brought large pans of precooked meals with her.

We went to the church service and then gave a fond good-bye to Kristi. Her parents took her home. Kristi was going to face a practically wrecked house. The people who had stayed there free of charge repaid Steve and Kristi's kindness by ruining the carpet, leaving human defecation and over a month's worth of trash in the garage with maggots crawling everywhere. They broke furniture and the air-conditioning. Steve and Kristi's cat was starving. The yard was a mess. Even a tree was dead because one of the kids had ripped the bark from it. Poor Kristi had to face all this alone.

In the meantime, we drove to Abilene to our next speaking engagement where we were to meet Gary Reisor, a friend from home and our first new traveling companion, along with several other friends who had driven from Fort Worth to see us. I played catch outside of Elmcrest Baptist Church with my boys right up until the time I had to meet the pastor. I missed being their coach!

I went into the pastor's study and talked with Brother Milton, the pastor. Afterwards, I saw my old friends the Smiths, Sharps, Leroys, and Gary. It was a real homecoming. We screamed and hugged each other before going into the service. John Sharp sang one of my favorite songs, "He Who Has Begun a Good Work in You," just before I spoke. It was a tremendously emotional service for me. I relived the horror of the accident, yet told of unspeakable joy in realizing God's love. They took up a love offering for us and I signed books before rushing to my next speaking engagement. After only two days, I said good-bye to my family again. They were leaving for Fort Worth.

I was driven to Tuscola Baptist Church by Dorothy, the pastor's wife. Steve and Gary loaded up the RowCycle and the RV with books. They would meet us there later. We arrived late as the music director let out a sigh of relief. I spoke for the third time that day. I was very tired, yet God spoke through me. After the service the pastor took us out to eat at the only restaurant in Tuscola.

"What's good here?" I asked.

"Well?" was the only response.

"What do you recommend?" Steve asked.

"Well?"

Gary, the engineer of the bunch, was going to cut through the red tape and come right to the point. "What are you having?" Gary asked, knowing he had them this time.

"Well, we're not eating, but you go ahead." And we did

We drove back to Abilene to the Royal Inn compliments of ElmCrest and stayed in the executive suite. As much as I needed sleep, I enjoyed talking with Gary, and I had a great time right up until the moment I discovered that I had a pressure sore. It was not large but could stop the trip if it went out of control. In addition, my kidney infection was growing worse, causing more tiredness than ever. I hoped I would make it home in time!

Day 43—Monday, May 14

We ate breakfast at the hotel in a plush restaurant. I assured Gary that we did not live like this every day. We drove to KRBC-TV for an interview. By 11, Gary drove us back to Albany. The wind was out of the southeast for the fourth day in a row. I should have been rested with a day off, but I was tired already.

After lunch we began rowing at 12:45. We passed through Breckenridge almost to Palo Pinto when suddenly a man jumped out of a car and began doing calisthenics. I thought he was a terrorist or an escapee from a mental ward as he continued to jump up and down and loosen up. Upon passing him, he looked familiar. I remembered meeting him at ElmCrest the night before. He was a Ph.D. Joe.

"Do you mind if I run along with you for a mile or so?" he asked."

"No, of course not, Doctor," I responded, honored that a man of his intelligence and training would want to tag along with me.

"Because I'm a doctor, Rob, I understand how hard it is both mentally and physically for you to walk. I've read your book and given two more to doctor friends of mine. You've inspired all of us never to give up on our goals in life."

We kept on talking as he ran two more miles with me. We exchanged praises to God before his wife picked him up. I could not believe what fabulous shape he was in. I was pleased to call him a friend.

I continued to row against the wind for another couple of hours before stopping at forty miles for the day just as a thunderstorm with tornado warnings approached and began to unleash its fury on us. We drove to Possum Kingdom Lake and camped beside it. The sight of lightning over the lake and high winds blowing through the trees was dramatic. Steve and I worked on the bike and RowCycle while Gary cooked dinner. Deer were walking around and were so tame that Steve even petted one.

The most unusual adventure of the day still remained as we tried to find a wheelchair-accessible bathroom in the darkness. Gary and I went ahead and Steve returned to the RV for towels. Gary and I groped through the darkness and passed two bathrooms without showers when we finally found one and waited for Steve. Steve located us minutes later but had the strangest look on his face.

"You guys will never believe what just happened to me. I was walking along the trail in the darkness when a deer walked right up to me, kind of spooking me. The deer smelled my pockets to see if I had anything for him. After discovering that I did not, he . . ."

"What, what did he do Steve?" I asked, hoping he was A-OK.

"He cleaned his nostrils on me. That's right, he used me as a handkerchief!"

We broke into laughter as we went into the showers and killed spiders that lay in wait for us in the stalls. Nature had turned against us. But neither spiders nor deer with runny noses could stop us (sounds like the slogan for the Post Office). The sky was filled with lightning and thunder all night. We were thankful for air-conditioning and dry beds. Zzzzzzz . .

Day 44—Tuesday, May 15

We rose at 6:30 AM to the fragrant aroma of Gary cooking a large breakfast of sausage and eggs. Steve lubricated the RowCycle and bike because of the hard rain. We began rowing by 8. It rained briefly, and lightning, thunder, and high winds continued until after lunch. We began hitting hills outside of Palo Pinto. It was only 11:30, but Gary had already done our laundry, cleaned the RV, and had lunch waiting for us. We stopped for the day outside of Mineral Wells and left the RV with afriends of ours. Wanice picked us all up, left me at her parents' home, and then carried Gary and Steve to their homes.

During the night, my temperature began to rise. The kidney infection was upon me, but, praise God, it had waited until I was home. Wanice was there to care for me.

Day 45—Wednesday, May 16

We were grateful that my kidney infection was mild. I rested while I was treated like a king by my in-laws. I exulted, "Hey, the worst part of the trip is over!" Brother and sister, was I wrong!

We drove to the next church in Weatherford. I shared my testimony with the church and met Johnny. He had broken his back, but had a much greater chance than I had of walking and was doing great, even though his accident had happened only a year before. I encouraged Johnny and the church to hang in there for Jesus.

Buddy, the pastor, escorted us to eat, gave us a love offering, and led us to Lake Mineral Wells State Park. We drove over the spillway. The water was dangerously high. It rushed over the spillway and cascaded down a waterfall to our left. There were no rails to keep us from going over. Gary and I held our breath as fearless Steve followed the pastor across. When we were right in the middle, Steve suddenly stopped.

"Look at this!" he cried.

We peered out in front of the RV, and there was the largest water moccasin we had ever laid eyes on. It was trapped on the spillway by the rushing water. No one volunteered to throw him back into the lake! We drove ahead to a secluded part of the park and were soon asleep.

Day 46—Thursday, May 17

We started at 8 in Mineral Wells and rowed through Weatherford while Gary tended to the RV and lunch. Youth ministers Brian and Steve came out to ride into Fort Worth with us. Several of our friends met us on the outskirts of the city. I also spoke to Jennifer Briggs French and Ron Jenkins with the Fort Worth paper.

We started out again at 5 PM with an entourage of cars and bikes. I was home! Friends began to drive by and honk. We rowed to Loop 820 where we were met by a police escort, then down Camp Bowie Boulevard. As I rowed down the familiar streets, memories of the first half of the trip flooded my mind—1,200 miles of desert, the eighty-mile day, eight miles without water, and El Capitan. Other memories returned as I relived the daily pain. Steve and I did not have to exchange words as we looked at each other, knowing we had done it together. Rather, *He* did it!

I approached the large parking lot where I was to meet the press and officially end rowing for the day. I looked ahead and saw 200 or 300 friends, fellow employees, and church members. CBS and local television filmed as the crowd applauded. Steve was by my side as we turned into the parking lot.

Dale Klugman, my boss, addressed the crowd and introduced Mayor

Pro-temp Gary Gilley and other dignitaries. I was presented with the key to Fort Worth (only three have ever been given out before; one to Astronaut Beane and the other to the *Voyager*). It was declared "Rob Bryant Day" in Fort Worth. It was not really my day, though. It was God's.

Days 47 and 48—Friday and Saturday, May 18 and 19

I rested for two days and nursed the kidney infection into remission. We had a party at our house with over fifty friends. Steve and Mack worked on the RowCycle for two days.

Steve was not tired at all! He returned a few tapes to a video store when he looked down only to discover that he was standing there in his underwear!

I played catch with my tired arms I could barely raise. It was a "labor of love" for the boys. I was presented with several checks for paralysis research, but mostly I rested.

Day 49—Sunday, May 20

I spoke to Rolling Meadows Baptist church in Arlington where Wanice had a surprise waiting for me. I met with Jerry Royale, the pastor (I felt extremely old—I had taught Jerry in Sunday School). We walked into the sanctuary. Wanice had an unusual smile on her face as she looked to our left and then back at me. There sitting toward the back were two familiar-looking people. I looked back at Wanice. She had tears in her eyes as I turned one more time to see if my eyes were deceiving me. I moved slowly toward the two men in the back. It was too good to be true. I stopped in fear that I was going to be disappointed. I began propelling myself again, walked past them, and pivoted.

I was looking into the eyes of the two men who had changed my life more than anyone except my father. There was Dave Koksma, who had led me to the Lord thirteen years before. I remembered the adventures we had in the military that had filled the first six chapters of *Lord, Lift Me Up* . . . . Jim Hurst was also there. He had helped me train every day for a year for the world-record "Miracle Walk." To testify it was an emotional service would be an understatement. That night I spoke to Southcliff, my home church. I spoke of the first part of my rowing across America. They gave a reception there that made the presidential inauguration look like a sock hop.

Days 50 and 51—Monday and Tuesday, May 21 and 22

I rested for the last time before the "Row Across America" was to begin again. We fixed the external damage to the RV and packed it with food and equipment. I spoke with as many of my friends as I possibly-could. I coordinated with Daphne Eley at work to schedule DynCorp speaking engagements, and I helped plan for three more months of my absence from work. All too soon, the time to leave home and family had again arrived.

(Left to Right) Rob, Wanice, Jonathan, and Jason

The first "Row Across America" team (Left to Right) Wanice, Rob, Steve, and Kristi.

Rowing on the first day—"Getting out of L.A. alive" with Steve, John, and Bruce.

Rob and Steve climbing Chiraco Summit in California.

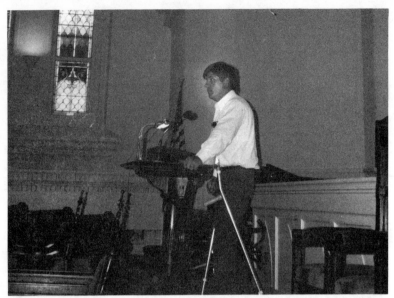

Rob spoke to Bardstown Baptist Church in Kentucky. Rob was recovering from a life-threatening kidney infection.

Rob and Don were filmed by NBC in Pittsburgh just days after the painful "wipeout" in Wheeling, West Virginia.

At Columbus AFB, Rob was about to race a T-38. He lost. Rob spoke at many military bases.

Rob took time to speak with children in Terrell, Texas.

Near Bald Lake Summit, the sign represented the next mile of five miles of dangerous curves and grades.

With five ridges behind him, Rob beheld his very first Washington, D.C., sign.

Steve, Lee, and Rob were halfway across America; little did Rob know that he will be stranded only two weeks later.

Rob and Steve were escorted by the sheriff of Warren County (MS) across the Mississippi River bridge.

(Left to Right) Bob Peterson, Don Bright, Wanice, and Rob in front of the Eternal Light Memorial at the Gettysburg battlefield.

(Left to Right) Dan Bannister, President of DynCorp, Rob, Chuck Lievrouw, and Dan DuBoise at a reception in Reston, Virginia.

The "Row Across America" team, minus two members, at the Capitol.

Rob posed with disabled spectators at the Capitol.

(Left to Right) Congressman Dyson, Sandy, Rob, Wanice and Admiral Boecker held up the flag flown over the Capitol in Rob's honor.

Rob gave all of the glory to God for the 3,280-mile "Guinness World Record"—at the Pennsylvania Avenue Baptist Church.

(Left to Right) Rob's father, Lee, and brothers Steve, Rob, Mike, and Rob Jr.

9

"Dad, I Still Remember"—
We Remember What We Are Taught

Day 52—Wednesday, May 23

The day's team consisted of our driver Dan Henninge, my brother Steve, and Steve the paraplegic on his arm-powered bike. We went down Camp Bowie Boulevard through thick to the Fort Worth Trinity River bike trails where I had trained for a year and a half. Because of flooding weeks before, the water was still awfully high. I was surprised that Steve was keeping up with us. He had trained for six weeks to accompany me on this day. I was proud of his accomplishment. Soon, we went right through downtown Fort Worth to Highway 80.

Then a peculiar thing happened. My brother Steve stopped at a store for Gatorade. Several minutes later, I looked to my side and saw that his bike was back. Suddenly I saw a large pistol hanging on his side. I turned to look closer when I realized it wasn't Steve. It was a policeman on a bike! I was obviously startled but hoped he had a sense of humor.

"Officer, was I speeding?"

He laughed and returned, "No, but can I see your registration please?"

He asked if he could escort me for awhile, and we were soon joined by two other policemen on bikes. When Steve caught up with us later, we were quite a sight: three police officers on bikes, one civilian on a bike, and two men on what-cha-ma-call-its.

My pressure sore was still a problem, so when my RoHo cushion (inflatable seat for paraplegics) went flat, we were done for the day. We had almost made it to Arlington. That night I spoke to Steve and Kristi's church. It was great to see Kristi again.

Day 53—Thursday, May 24

At 6:30 AM we drove to the starting point in Arlington and rowed toward Dallas. For the next three days the team consisted of four people. Wanice was driver and cook; Gerald Bell (a good friend) rode a bike and helped Steve. Of course, the ever-faithful Steve rode his bike at my side. Traffic was heavy as we approached downtown and crossed a major bridge with no shoulder. It required over five minutes to cross the bridge. Not one car passed us during the lunch traffic hour. What a miracle! We finished for the day at the Dallas City Hall and jumped into the RV.

We drove to Dallas Rehabilitation Institute (DRI) for a reception there hosted by the National Paralysis Foundation and was emceed by Kent Waldrep, president of that organization. Media included CBS, KRLD radio, and local television. I spoke to the paraplegics and quadriplegics and told them they had challenges ahead of them, but with God's help, there was no mountain too tall. I was inducted as the first person to go into the Circle of Honor at DRI. I was met by Cliff Harris (an ex-Dallas Cowboy) and with a proclamation from Dallas Mayor Annette Strauss naming it "Row Across America Day." Then I was interviewed by David Gold of KLIF radio and met Fort Worth Mayor Bob Bolen. I returned home for the final time. I spent as much time with Jason and Jonathan as I could. Tomorrow Daddy was leaving home again for ten weeks.

Day 54—Friday, May 25

We started rowing at the Dallas City Hall at 8:15 AM. It was very dangerous in downtown Dallas on several roads parallel to Highway 80. Buses, trucks, and cars whipped by us and we had several close calls as people recognized us from the media and were not as careful as they should have been. The wind was out of the east again. We left Dallas for Mesquite, Forney, and Terrell.

As we approached Terrell, Steve saw a ladder lying on the side of the road. He stopped and examined it. It was in perfect condition.

"Rob, do you mind if I take this along? I need a good ladder."

I thought he was kidding, of course, so I said sure. I continued rowing as he tied it like a wing onto his bike. He was serious! He was going to carry the ladder six miles to the RV. Gerald and I went on ahead. However, as soon as Steve started, he had a flat tire. Gerald and I were met by some media and a small busload of kids at the Terrell Chamber of Commerce. After they left, we tried contacting Steve by radio. No Steve! We waited for another half hour and were about to load up the RV and search for him when he pulled into the parking lot looking like a B-29. He tied the ladder to the top of the RV, and then we all ate lunch. Steve told us about the problem he had crossing bridges with no shoulders. But Steve was like his older brother: hard-headed and never say *quit!*

After an hour break, we rowed eighteen more miles to Wells Point and were met by a reporter from Canton. We had gone fifty miles for the day. I was amazed at how much the four-day break had refreshed me. We were in bed by 10. Steve returned from calling Kristi, and we were all asleep. That's when the "snore" festivities began. Gerald was snoring so loud that the wall of the RV seemed to be moving in and out. Steve tried waking him several times, but within minutes Gerald was snoring again. Besides, by the time Steve exerted the energy to shove Gerald, he (good ole Steve) couldn't go back to sleep. Finally, Steve had an idea. He hung one of the two-way radios beside Gerald's ear and then got one for himself. Steve waited until Gerald began snoring again and then yelled "Gerald" into the radio. Gerald immediately sat straight up in bed and looked around. He couldn't see anyone awake so he went back to sleep. Steve repeated this as many times as necessary during the night. Steve told Gerald about it the next morning. The "snore story" would be the joke of the week.

Day 55—Saturday, May 26

We were rowing by 7:45. Gerald was very sore sitting on the seat of his bike and asked Steve, "How have you done this for 1,600 miles?"

We passed through the Texas hill country and hit large hills outside of Grand Saline. Just as we were approaching Canton, several bikes shot past us. We found ourselves in the middle of a bike race. Riders were passing us like we were standing still. One lady stopped and asked us what kind of time we were making in the race.

I said, "Well, for the past 1,600 miles my speed has been only eight or nine miles an hour."

She thought I was just kidding and asked me again. I explained what we were doing. She was so impressed that she gave us a donation for paralysis research and almost cried as she saw me struggling along through the hills.

After going twenty-eight miles, we stopped for lunch at a park outside Mineola. Wanice had fixed salad, spaghetti, fruit, and bread. After lunch we passed a desk on the side of the road and Steve looked at me as if he were wondering if he could carry it back to the RV like he had the ladder.

"Forget it, Steve," I quickly replied. He pretended to load the desk onto his bike before rejoining us.

We encountered more hills before we finished forty-eight miles at 4:30 outside Longview. We drove back to Forney to meet Wanice's parents. They were bringing Jason and Jonathan to spend a day with me before I left the area. Steve and Wanice waited at the meeting point while Gerald and I went to stalk the wild hamburger. That's when we met Max, no doubt a caring, loving person—but also persistent.

As soon as we pulled up, he jumped out of his car and ran over to examine the RowCycle hanging on the back of the RV. Gerald was picking up the food as Max walked right into the RV and asked me what I was doing. It kind of stunned me that he would walk in without being invited, but Max was full of surprises.

"Are you the guy who's rowing across America? Well, of course you are. Boy, it's a pleasure meeting you. I want you to meet my family."

He leaned out of the door and called for his folks to come in. They paused for a moment at the door.

"He doesn't mind if you come in. Do you, Rob? No, of course you don't! Come on in! Hey, this guy is setting a Guinness World Record among other things . . ." Before I could say anything, the entire family was aboard. I shook hands with them as Max kept on talking. He talked nonstop for ten minutes. Gerald had come back by then, and we were trying to figure a polite way of excusing ourselves when Max made us an offer.

"Hey, I've got a great idea. You can stay with us tonight. You can park in our driveway. I have hook-ups and extra bedrooms. We'll talk all night! Why, we can . . ."

I politely told him we would think about it. He jotted down his address before we left. We were very touched by his generosity but knew we probably wouldn't get any sleep if we stayed there. We felt ashamed that we were relieved to have escaped Max. We drove the RV back to the meeting place just as Wanice's parents were arriving with the boys. Guess who else pulled up? Max!! We couldn't believe it. He had followed us. He went on for another ten minutes straight about the accommodations and how much fun we were going to have. He wanted us to follow him home right then, but somehow we got away, telling him that we would consider his offer. We once again felt ashamed as we tried to elude Max by driving as fast as possible back to the same RV park outside of Forney where we had stayed the night before.

Upon arriving, we showered. That's when Max's pursuit continued. Steve finished his shower first and walked over to the door to leave. He opened the door and paused before asking, "Max, what brings you here?" He had followed us again! Gerald and I were dumb-struck as we peered out of the shower toward the door. All we saw was Steve standing there with an "I-gotcha" look. It worked! Gerald and I were passing out over the prospect of an evening with Max. This was the same RV park where Steve had used the "how-to-stop-snoring radio technique" on Gerald. For the next several days, Gerald not only kept his eyes open for the return of Max, he would not snore around Steve again! Max, wherever you are, you are a truly hospitable soul. God bless you.

We were in bed early because the team was going to be changing the next day. Wanice, Gerald, and the boys were leaving, and my father and stepmother were on their way to relieve them. I was so excited about seeing my parents that I could barely sleep.

Day 56—Sunday, May 27

After breakfast, Steve drove us to a Baptist Church in Terrell. After the service, we ate at a restaurant directly across from the church. I sat on pins and needles waiting to see my father and stepmother, Jane. Just as the meal started, Dad and Jane came walking into the restaurant to meet us. We squealed with excitement.

After the meal, Wanice, Jason, Jonathan, and Gerald prepared to go home. I kissed Wanice and the boys and shook Gerald's hand. I was so thankful for my family and good friends who were always there for me.

Little did I know that Gerald's best friend would come to my rescue just three weeks later in the greatest emotional challenge of the trip!

Steve drove the latest "Row Across America" team to a Baptist Church in Longview. We were interviewed by the media there. I also met Bob and Sandra Shaw. Bob was a T-12 paraplegic also but was restricted to the wheelchair. I had met many handicapped people across America, but Bob and I had an immediate rapport.

It was difficult for Dad to sit in church and relive the horror of my testimony. I was always emotional when I talked about walking for the first time after the accident. It tore up Dad and me each time. I knew by experience that until the children are parents themselves, they never understand how bad the parents hurt right along with the children. As a matter of fact, they would rather suffer themselves than see their children suffer. But he was so proud of me for never calling it quits. Dad also knew all too well that I would never give up rowing across America. It scared him that I was prepared to go to any physical and emotional extremes to finish, but he understood my drive. He had it, too!

That night in Longview, we stayed with Marla and Dwaine Pope, old friends of ours. It was Marla's birthday so we celebrated together. It rained all night as a bad storm passed.

Day 57—Monday, May 28

Dad drove the RV for the first time to our start point west of Longview. Since it was Dad's maiden voyage, it was a little scary, but we made it. It turned out that Kristi and Wanice were our most careful drivers. It was an overcast, cool day, but very humid. We were rowing by 7:30 AM. The hills were relentless and were from half a mile to one-and-a-half-miles long. They were becoming larger and steeper as we continued across the Texas hill country.

Heavy, green, dense brush covered the ground beneath tall pine and oak trees. At the bottoms of the hills, crickets and insects were deafening, and the heat and humidity increased. On the hilltops, birds were singing, and a light easterly breeze was blowing.

I had already had innumerable close calls with cars and trucks. Cars coming close no longer bothered me. I have truck-driver friends and appreciate what their eighteen-wheelers do, but in my situation, they could make me a mite nervous.

But within one hour this day, I was almost hit by three cars in a row. It did tick me off that with two lanes, the cars wouldn't move over. Because I am a Texan, I can get by with this: the worst drivers we met were in Texas. At one point Steve dropped back to fill my water container. I could see him in my mirror just as he was almost hit by an eighteen-wheeler. The truck then went way around me.

The hours slowly passed and by lunchtime, we were in Longview. We stopped in a church parking lot for lunch, joined by a reporter, Marla, and her three children. After a one-hour hiatus, we began again. Dad and Jane did the shopping and made phone calls and meals. We finished for the day at 4 with forty-eight miles at a roadside park almost to the Louisiana border. We drove back to the Popes's house for one more night.

While heading in that direction, Steve saw that my lips were cracking and turned to Jane, "Mom," he called her. "Mom, I think Rob needs something for his lips." I wondered if he meant a motherly kiss."

I also wondered what was going to happen, but as I opened my mouth to speak, a large tablespoon of vegetable oil was crammed into it. Steve would repeat this several times a day. As much as I hated to admit it, the oil did heal my chapped and bleeding lips. But I declared that I would have my revenge on Steve and Jane.

Day 58—Tuesday, May 29

We left the Popes's home for the final time at 7:15 AM after another huge breakfast. I was rowing by 8, but for the first time since Fort Worth, I did not want to row. I had about "had it." I was thankful that I had decided before beginning the trip that I would never quit no matter what, because on days like this, I might have. The only question was how far, not whether or not to row.

As we approached Louisiana, the hills lessened somewhat, but in my tired condition they were all mountains. The trees were taller, with long vines bigger around than my leg hanging from them. We noticed that when the vines grew too large they would actually crush the trees. It reminded me of how sin starts like a small vine, but grows until it is big and heavy enough to break a person's relationship with God.

Just before the border, Highway 80 came to an end, so we accessed the interstate. After lunch I began rowing again. Somehow I was about as tired as I had ever been. How could I go on rowing five or six days a week and speaking two to four times on my supposed days off? I was encouraged by a handicapped lady who stopped and said, "I'm so proud of you!" Isn't it wonderful how God sends His Barnabases (encouragers) to our rescue. Soon after, several cars passed with applauding passengers.

Steve and I paused at the Louisiana border to snap photos. I turned and looked back behind me. We had just crossed all 972 miles of Texas! I thought back to El Capitan on the other side of the state. It had almost done us in. As tough as the Texas terrain is, God is tougher!

Dad and Jane crossed the Louisiana border and drove to the ten-mile marker on the interstate. It would mark thirty-seven miles for the day. But more important, it was exactly halfway across America! The ground was much flatter, but I was exhausted as I continued to row. We crested the top of a hill and there they were: the RV, the marker, and the halfway point. I continued to pull on the handles until there was no strength left. Up ahead I could see Dad and Jane. I looked at my Dad. Suddenly in my mind's eye, Dad was not standing by the RV; he was standing on the top of Fort McHenry. I went back in memory to an event from my childhood that would change my way of thinking forever.

"Bang, bang, you're dead," I yelled.

"You missed," my older brother Mike yelled as he returned fire and ran for cover behind a huge 150-year-old cannon.

Mike and I were holding replicas of 1812 pistols and playing army in a "real live fort." For a seven-year-old boy, there wasn't a better place to play army than Fort McHenry. The old walls of the fort rose above us like mountains of rock. Mike and I ran up a flight of stairs out of the coolness of the rock fortress into the sunlight. Just then an elderly woman walked between us, and we both opened fire on her. At ages eight and seven, everybody was fair game in war. Suddenly, a shadow appeared over us, and we looked up at Dad towering over us. He peered down at us with a strange look on his face. Was it sadness? Why was he sad?

"Boys, I'm glad you're having a good time, but I'm afraid you're missing the point of our visit here. Come with me, Boys."

We followed him to the top of Fort McHenry. He pointed to the flag of the United States of America, to which we had "pledged allegiance" in school and church. It was flying proudly over the fort.

"Boys, there's a story behind that flag. We're going to take a trip in time together. Look behind you. That is the United States of America. The year is 1814. Washington, D.C., has been totally destroyed by the most powerful fighting force on earth—the British. Hundreds of Americans are either dead or homeless. Now that fighting force is on its way here. Several American fighting men form a living blockade to stop the British from taking the fort by land. Now, turn around and look the other way. That is the Chesapeake Bay. It leads to the Atlantic Ocean. The bay has been blocked off by British ships. The men in the fort are badly outnumbered and prepare to do battle on land and sea. Only a few hundred men are in the fort. But they promised one another that they would fight until the last one was dead before giving up. Well, the battle began with the cannons and rockets . . ."

My mind returned to the present as I crossed the halfway point with Steve by my side and Dad clapping. Dad was older and grayer. But to me he was as tall as ever. I turned to Dad and said, "Thanks, Dad." He seemed to understood exactly what I was feeling. No one had to tell me how fortunate I was to have such a supportive family.

The rest of the memory of Fort McHenry would return during a few tough times. I realized that my strength came from my Heavenly Father. But my earthly father still gave me something that would spur me on when I needed it, because what happened at Fort McHenry changed my life. Even more so, what happened at Calvary changed my life *forever!*

We celebrated a moment before loading up and driving to Holiday RV Park. It was the perfect place to celebrate. We were surrounded by flowers and tall trees. It was a well-deserved paradise. I lay in the pool while Dad and Jane washed our clothes in what seemed to be the oldest washer in the world. We ate supper and had a halfway party. Among the festivities was eating watermelon. Steve laid out all of his change and tools that he had picked up on the first half of the trip. I was amazed that he had about 100 tools, thirty-five dollars in change, and a ladder to show for it. Steve and I reminisced about our adventures with Dad and Jane.

I was excited about our accomplishment so far and the prospect of taking the next day off. The trip across Louisiana and Mississippi was going to be relatively flat. But the two Hs were going to be a tremendous challenge: Heat and Humidity. The hottest, most humid, rainiest days still lay ahead.

Day 59—Wednesday, May 30

Man, what a delight! Steve and I slept until 9:30 and then ate a leisurely breakfast outside, taking our time. We left the RV park around 11 as it began to rain. We drove to a hotel compliments of a nearby church. We rested until 4 and then ate at a place called Bodacious Barbecue. For what we were trying, we surely did need to be bodacious. I spoke at the church. We drove back to the hotel in the rain. It would rain nine out of the next fourteen days. Steve's back began hurting and would ache all during the rain, but he never complained. We were asleep by 11 PM.

Day 60—Thursday, May 31

I was up at 5:30 in the morning ready to pump out the miles. We ate breakfast at a restaurant. When it was time to pay, Dad wouldn't let me. As a matter of fact, they paid for most of our food and expenses for the entire week. I had already spent twenty-five thousand dollars, and the amount was growing! But God had led me in this venture, so I considered it a part of being faithful with my Christian stewardship.

We started rowing at 7:30 in the rain. I tried wearing my rain suit at first, but I was so hot and sweaty underneath, that I peeled it off and rowed without it. Steve and I marveled at the thick, jungle-like vegetation all around us. It rained off and on all day. Louisiana had already received so much rain that there was water near flood stage everywhere. We continued through Shreveport on Highway 80. The newspaper people came out exactly as we were crossing the Red River bridge. The pictures were on the wire services across the country. In the meantime, two of the three networks searched all over for us, but because of the short notice and intense rain, they never found us. We were later told it was like the Keystone Cops as they tried to find us. I'm disappointed they didn't.

As we passed through Bossier City, it rained so hard we could barely see. I put the rain suit on again, but it was more trouble than it was worth. I was soaked. Between rainstorms, it was so misty and dark that our visibility was drastically reduced. We were afraid of being run down before the driver saw us. Steve and I kept an eye on our mirrors all day. According to the radio, there were tornadoes in the area, but Steve and I were like two kids—yelling and screaming and having too much fun to worry about our safety. It was time for some more fun. Steve and I assumed the personalities of two otters.

Dad and Jane found a suitable place for a lunch stop, and they radioed their location to us. We topped a small hill, and there they were on the other side of the four-lane highway. It was difficult to see them because of the rain and mist, but they were visible. They were right beside a crossover, so it would not be demanding to maneuver across to them. Just then, Dad's voice came over the radio.

"I see you boys. We're on the lefthand side of the road. Can you see us?"

Steve and I looked at each other. Another game was about to begin—the "I-can't-see-you" game. Steve radioed back and said we could not see them. We continued along the road, pretending to be looking all over for them.

Dad was frantic! He gave us his position several times. He was right beside us as we passed and pretended to be furiously looking for him. It was raining on his boys, and they were lost! He probably wondered how we had made it this far across America.

"Boys, you're passing me right now. Can't you see us?"

We kept on going right past him looking everywhere but in the right direction. Now Dad was getting mad.

"You guys are blind! I'm right here. This is crazy!"

"Dad, we don't appreciate you hiding from us like this," I returned.

Now Dad was fit to be tied. We went almost out of sight as Dad continued yelling at us to turn around. We turned at the next crossover, and then practically ran into the back of the RV still claiming that we could not see him. Dad finally figured out that we were only kidding him and he laughed for days about the incident. Anyhow, he never again made the mistake of asking us if we could see him again.

As we ate, the rain intensified. We did not want to leave the warmth and comfort of the RV, but we could wait no longer. We were rowing again by 1:30. I left my rain suit off and never wore it again. It was better to be drenched by the cool rain then be trapped inside the suit. Steve and I watched for funnel clouds. The rain was so hard and lightning so close that we could barely hear each other. Several times, we saw trees blowing in circles. We should have stopped for the day, but the storm was too exciting to miss.

A large van pulled up beside us, and the driver asked us if we wanted to come in out of the rain. I answered no and began talking about our trip as I sat there in the RowCycle and almost drowned. The driver pointed to the side of the van with "First Baptist Church of Minden, Louisiana." One of my messages was scheduled for there, so the driver knew all about us. He offered us shelter one more time and then left, wondering what kind of crazy guest speaker was coming. He probably thought I didn't have enough sense to get in out of the rain.

We stopped for the day with over forty miles rowed, at the bottom of a hill outside Minden. I could go no further. We were wet, cold, tired, and—you guessed it—extremely hungry. The Chamber of Commerce directed us to a free night's lodging at the fairgrounds. We parked there, and a couple of groundskeepers helped us hook up to the electricity and water, assisted by Dad.

"Be careful outside in the rain," Jane told Dad.

"I'll be OK. I've been rained on before," he said as he stepped outside Just then a bolt of lightning hit right next to the RV. Suddenly the door opened and Dad sprang back in.

"Well, maybe I'll wait a minute for the weather to clear up."

The rain continued until 8 PM. While it rained, we hung up our clothes and talked the hours away. Finally the rain stopped, and the most vivid rainbow appeared in the twilight sky.

I was glad that Dad had been there for the halfway point. He built us up as only a good parent can. He and Jane were departing soon, but they were leaving a part of themselves behind with us.

10

Superwoman to the Rescue—
Strength Comes from the Ones We Love

Day 61—Friday, June 1

Rowing by 7:45, Steve and I climbed a steep hill through Minden. Within minutes, we were out in the country again. I was impressed with trees so thick that the houses appeared to be carved out of them. There was every color of green imaginable. We passed several abandoned homes. They were completely overtaken by brush and trees, almost making them invisible from the road only feet away.

It was no longer a mystery to me why there are so many furniture manufacturers in this area. We passed several sawmills and dense forests. It seemed that every other truck carried tons of raw lumber. We caused several traffic jams as these giant trucks slowed down to pass us. Because there was no shoulder, this was indeed a dangerous situation for Steve and me. We passed through Gibbsville and ate lunch in Arcadia in front of a grocery store. While I rested, Steve worked on a few new squeaks on the RowCycle. I did not want to start after lunch. By 1:30 we were going again. The air was so humid and heavy that it was hard to breathe. Getting winded in the thick, stale air was a constant challenge. The temperature was almost 100 with nearly 100-percent humidity. The lowlands were marshlike with loud insects. Nearby hills were covered with trees. It seemed like we were on a different planet from the desert. Our surroundings had changed from extreme aridity to extreme humidity.

At 3 we passed a university that stands for the Deep South—Grambling State. Steve fixed a spring on the RowCycle right before we stopped for the day at 39.2 miles, just outside Ruston. Wanice, Jason, Jonathan, and Steve were going to be the final "Row Across America" team before Kristi's return.

Within an hour Wanice and the boys pulled up and met us on the side of the road. My sweetie brought boxes of food for the next several weeks. We drove to an RV park outside of Ruston. It was covered with stately trees and fishing ponds. It also had a wheelchair-accessible bathroom.

Steve and I bade farewell to Dad and Jane, who planned on leaving in the morning before we woke up. I was so thankful they had come. He was responsible for giving all three of his boys courage and determination.

Day 62—Saturday, June 2

We were awake at 7, rowing by 8:15. Our surroundings were changing from dense forest to farming communities. We were leaving one steamy forest but had several more ahead before Tennessee, more than 500 miles away. We took a break after seventeen miles and started again. I was amazed that I was able to row sometimes all morning or afternoon without stopping one time. I credit two things for this:

1. I had lost fifteen pounds and was in terrific shape. My arms were over seventeen inches around, and my chest measured almost fifty inches. But the second thing I could not take credit for:

2. The hills were smaller!

Often, Steve and I would row and bike all day without saying anything. Steve was a quiet man, and besides, I was grunting and often too out of breath to talk anyway. Steve did not waste words. He saved them for when he had something important to say! So when Steve talked, I listened. We were moving along up a slight grade when I heard a very deep guttural "woof" coming from a home on our left. We had already seen every variety of dog imaginable. Since we were moving along at eight miles per hour, we had become personally acquainted with every barking dog between Los Angeles and Louisiana. I very casually looked over to see what kind of canine it was this time. I was horrified to behold the largest Great Dane I had ever seen racing toward us with his teeth bared. Most Great Danes are docile, but this one had not heard that. The dog was actually taller than I was, in my sitting position. If he reached me, he could do a lot of damage.

Steve was not in a great position to defend himself, either. He was behind me when he leaned forward and uttered three words, "Rob, row faster!" He did not have to tell me twice. I was pulling on the handles as hard as I could. I ignored the pain, thinking of the alternative. Just then a car passed us, cutting off the path of the dog. We were over the hill in no time. I wondered if I could have made better time had the dog been with us since California.

We went another nine miles before lunch in Calhoun. After lunch we continued through the countryside. We could hear a train in the distance. As it drew closer, it blew its whistle. The lonely muffled sound echoed through the forest. The mournful wail appeared to be miles away in another dimension of time. We moved into a clearing. The forest had been so thick that it had muted the deafening sound of the train passing within 100 feet of us on the right.

The country slowly turned into city as we passed through Calhoun to Claiborne and finally into West Monroe. After another twelve miles, we stopped at 3:00 after thirty-eight miles for the day. We drove to the Bastrop Inn compliments of a Baptist Church in Bastrop. The rooms were large condominium style. After so long in the RV, we marveled that we could touch only one wall at a time.

Day 63—Sunday, June 3

We had an absolutely incredible service. Jim Taylor, the pastor, was kind to us. Steve sang and I spoke. The church was moved and even took up a love offering for us. There were several handicapped people there. One was so severely handicapped that he used a "See and Spell" to communicate. He asked me if I could help him find a new wife. His had left him. I was so thankful that Wanice had stayed with me through thick and thin. I had given Wanice the option to leave me after my accident. I loved her enough to let her go if she wanted. She thought I was speaking Greek to her. I often get credit for my courage and determination. But the truth is that Wanice is always behind the scenes giving me the encouragement I need. I bought her a Valentine that said it all several years before. It was an elephant walking on a tightrope. I put my name on the elephant. But when the card is opened, there is a canary offstage flying backwards holding the tightrope in its beak. I put Wanice's name on the canary. In short, our friends know that mild-mannered Wanice is really Superwoman.

We ate lunch with the pastor and his family. It rained all day . . . (sounds like "Oh, Susannah," doesn't it?) as we drove back to Bossier City for the next service. It was a two-hour drive to what we discovered was one of the smallest churches of the trip, but it was important for me to be there. I pray that I blessed the people as they blessed me.

Back in West Monroe near the start point, it hit me like a wet mackerel and I sighed heavily. We were now entering the busiest three weeks of the trip. In addition to rowing 600 more miles, I would need to speak twenty-five times in the next nineteen days!

Day 64—Monday, June 4

We woke at 6:15 AM and were rowing by 7:45 through West Monroe and then through Monroe itself. CBS came out to film us. In addition to the media, a vanload of the congregation and the pastor from Cherry Ridge Baptist church came out to cheer us on.

We stopped for the day because of a speaking engagement at lunchtime. We ate outside a few old abandoned buildings that Jason and Jonathan just knew were a "ghost town." Steve drove us back to Minden to the Louisiana Rehabilitation Center, and we ate lunch a second time. Fantastic! I was escorted around the hospital and tried to inspire the patients that they could accomplish their dreams. I saw a young man lifting weights half-heartedly in physical therapy. It reminded me of myself several years before facing the horror of the unknown in a wheelchair. I shared my testimony with him. He began lifting weights in earnest! Soon after, I met Tyrone, a seventeen-year-old quadriplegic. He was a Christian and had a tremendous attitude considering such a debilitating injury.

"A person does not have to look far to realize how lucky he is," Tyrone said with a smile. I would see how right he was later that night! I addressed the entire hospital staff and patients in a large room. I believe all of them were encouraged. The patients saw what was possible if they worked hard enough and only believed. The staff saw that their work was not always in vain.

We drove to First Baptist Church in Minden. After eating supper with the church family, I spoke to a congregation in the family life center. NBC filmed me as I spoke to them. That's when I met John. He was twenty-eight, a C-2 quadriplegic on life-support machines. A tear ran down our cheeks as we talked with each other. His attitude was that he was thankful to be alive. I felt ashamed for ever complaining about anything.

"John, as I am climbing the Appalachians toward the end of the trip, I am going to be thinking of you," I said. "John, if you can face your challenges, I can face mine. I am going to climb those mountains for both of us!"

We were escorted to a hotel, compliments of First Baptist, Minden.

Day 65—Tuesday, June 5

We woke at 6 and were rowing by 7:30. We rowed through Delhi with many people waving to us. We passed a few little boys playing, and one of them screamed, "Hey, there goes the guy who's rowing across America!"

Soon after, we passed through Tallulah, and more people waved. We would find that more and more people recognized us the farther we went. A man pulled up beside us and asked, "Are you giving autographs? My son read about you in *My Weekly Reader*." I signed his little book before moving on. We stopped under a few large trees for lunch and ate watermelon for dessert. Steve and I grew extremely thirsty each day, and could eat half a watermelon at a time—each. The temperature was close to 100 with over 90-percent humidity by the afternoon. The heat zapped our energy. We found ourselves drinking over a quart of water per hour. We stopped for the day at forty miles outside Delhi. We were close to the Mississippi River. We drove back to Delhi First Baptist Church, took baths, and ate pounds of Wanice's lasagna. We spoke on the ACTS Christian television network, and a few reporters visited with us.

We drove towards Vicksburg and crossed the Mississippi River. We saw the aftermath of a terrible accident as we crossed the bridge. We also noticed that there was no shoulder with signs that said: *No Bikes Allowed*. We were obviously going to need help when we crossed the bridge on the RowCycle! We continued driving to Vicksburg to a lush, green campground.

We were all in bed early. I prayed for guidance about the bridge.

Day 66—Wednesday, June 6

I finally had a day off from rowing, but I had three speaking engagements involving televison, radio, and a church. My fat was almost gone, my hands hurt, and my back and shoulders were sore. I wondered how I was going to continue when I remembered John. I stopped thinking negatively immediately!

Among other phone calls, I called the chief of police in Vicksburg. I was told the chief was going to come personally to insure our safety. He knew all too well how dangerous the bridge was. Before the interviews were to begin, we took a few hours to drive through Civil War Military Parkway in Vicksburg. I was overwhelmed at the loss of life there. There was statue after statue of men who went to their graves fighting for what they believed. These men who had died so bravely gave me the courage to continue.

We drove back to Rayville (Louisiana) to the radio interview and then to Monroe for a church service. We went to a hotel, compliments of a local Baptist Church, and ate supper. We raced to the 6 PM service and then went immediately to an hour-long interview with Charles Reed on the local Christian television station.

At 10:30, we drove back to the hotel for a second supper with pastor Dwaine Duncan. He told us how he was asked to be the pastor of his church. I had already spoken to seventy-six churches and had heard miracle after miracle, but this story was truly amazing.

Pastor Duncan explained, "God had given the name of Duncan to the pulpit committee chairman. The chairman drove to the neighboring town of Duncanville in hopes that he would find the pastor there. After all, the name Duncan is in the name Duncanville. After a church service there, the chairman went to a restaurant with a pastor hoping he could find his man. While the chairman was eating, he was introduced to me. I told him my name was Duncan. I was between churches. Guess what? I was called immediately!"

Day 67—Thursday, June 7

We left the hotel by 6:15 AM and drove all the way back to our start point by the Mississippi River bridge. We were rowing by 8:30. We rowed to the bridge and waited for the police. Within a few minutes, up pulled the Vicksburg polive chief and a patrolman. We slowly made our way across the dangerous bridge with the aid of the police escort and arrived at Mississippi Visitors Center at 9:15. We were met by several members of the press. Among them was a writer for the Vicksburg paper who also happened to be a member of Bowmar Avenue Baptist Church. I was to speak there the next Sunday. I was introduced to the Warren County sheriff and several other police officers who then escorted us through town. They told us to stay on I-20 because it was less hilly and much safer than the alternate route.

We proceeded down the interstate hoping to exit onto Hwy 80 several miles down the road. However, four miles later a patrolman told us to get off the road and go back several miles to another route that would lead us to 80. Steve and I explained to him what we were doing and began to pray that we would not have to go back. He paused suddenly and told us to wait. He walked back to his car and used his radio. Steve and I held our breath, hoping that we had not gone miles out of our way. He returned, "Fellows, I shouldn't do this, but go ahead. Exit up ahead at the Highway 80 sign. I don't have time to escort you, and there are some narrow bridges ahead without shoulders. Be careful! But, if I see you on the interstate after that exit, I'll give you a ticket."

Steve and I didn't have to be told twice.

"Steve, I hope the police up ahead are as nice as all the policemen we have met here today."

I would soon find out differently.

We began to pray about the bridges that stretched out before us. Just as we saw the first bridge up ahead, a car pulled over. It was the pastor of Bowmar Avenue Baptist Church in Vicksburg. He just happened to pass by on his way to the hospital. He gave us an escort across three narrow bridges with no shoulders. The next ramp was our exit. Once again, God's timing was perfect.

We stopped for lunch in a parking lot and entered Highway 80. We talked about the fact that we accessed this route in West Texas over 1,200 miles ago. Furthermore, we would be on it almost to Birmingham. It was a small, winding, hilly route, but the alternative meant a ticket. Soon after beginning again, I took the lead, and Steve stopped to look at something. I noticed a stick lying on the right side of the road and swerved to go around it. Suddenly, the stick moved. It was a huge snake. Even though I passed within feet of it, it stood its ground. This was his road! I glanced in my mirror, and Steve was close behind.

"Steve, check out that stick back there."

Steve moved toward it, then suddenly swerved. He almost jumped off of his bike to avoid the snake. After regaining his balance, Steve yelled at me through the radio.

After several more tough hills, we stopped outside of Jackson with over forty miles for the day. We drove to an RV Park. Steve, the boys, and I went swimming while Wanice did all our laundry. Steve worked on the RowCycle and bike before we all went to bed at 9 PM.

Day 68—Friday, June 8

After breakfast, we started rowing again at 8:30. We traveled Highway 80 through downtown Jackson past the State Capitol. Local newspaper people met us and took pictures. Steve happened to meet a nurse as we passed the Jackson Rehabilitation Center. She would be instrumental in setting up a time for me to speak there later that week. Soon after, we entered Highway 25. It would prove to be the most dangerous road we had been on thus far. Wanice had lunch ready for us as usual. We went another eighteen miles after lunch despite the sweat and pain of rowing in 98-degree air with 95-percent humidity.

While I rowed, Wanice did laundry, went to the bank, and filled the tank with gas. The boys were busy helping her but sometimes were more help than she wanted. Jonathan opened the refrigerator door while they were moving; everything fell out. She even had time to find an RV park for us that night. She swung back and picked us up. We were ready to stop for the day after forty-three miles of sweating. Wanice drove us to Timberlake RV park. It had over one hundred RV and camping sites. We parked by the lake. It was one of the most beautiful parks on the entire trip. There was ample shade with birds singing and hundreds of campers scurrying everywhere. All of us went swimming and took showers. The excitement for the evening began when Jonathan walked back from the pool alone and got lost. We searched for him, but he calmly walked around until he saw me looking for him. He was lost for close to twenty minutes, yet he was mighty brave.

To rebuild my strength daily, I naturally ate more than ever before in my life. This time our family ate at a picnic table. Wanice and I watched an awesome sunset while talking with the boys. I was sad that my week with the family was almost over. I struggled to stay awake as long as possible with Jason and Jonathan before falling asleep at 10 PM.

Day 69—Saturday, June 9

It was so hot and I was so tired that I just put my mind in neutral and ignored the pain and heat. The hours slowly passed. Steve realized how tired I was and wished he could help me, but I was on my own to pull on the handles stroke after stroke, hill after hill, and mile after mile. The hills were becoming steeper and longer. The shoulder on Highway 25 dissipated to nothing, and the traffic was jam-packed. Steve and I had several close calls. What made it even more dangerous was: in order to overcome the pain, I had to ignore my surroundings and was semi-comatose. Steve watched the traffic for both of us. Often he had to yell to get my attention. We went fifteen more miles before stopping at 1 for the day. Somehow, we had covered thirty-five miles in the five hours of intense pain and concentration. Wanice had our lunch ready and drove for three hours back to Vicksburg while Steve and I ate and slept.

We went to a hotel compliments of Bowmar Avenue. After baths, Wanice, I, and the boys went out to a quiet restaurant and ate seafood by the Mississippi River. It was to be our last time together until Washington, D.C. I missed them already. Jason and Jonathan were going to miss me, but they explained that they were not going to miss living in an RV. They wanted to go home and play with their toys and friends.

Kristi arrived after a ten-hour drive in our car. She was tired and had news for me about her condition. Steve and Kristi celebrated by eating together and talked for hours about what all had happened since they saw each other last. We all met in my room and exchanged greetings and hugs before going to sleep. I was so tired, yet I slept for only four hours because I knew my family was leaving.

Day 70—Sunday, June 10

Wanice and I said good-bye over breakfast. We didn't know it, but we would be seeing each other long before Washington, D.C.

With pangs in my heart, I watched them drive away. Jonathan cried as they drove out of sight.

Steve, Kristi, and I arrived at Bowmar Avenue early enough to attend Sunday School. The teacher was talking about the tongue and the damage it could do. This was a message anyone could learn from, especially someone speaking to as many churches as I was. But then he made a few comments totally out of the scope of the lesson.

"Never give up a dream God has given you, regardless of the circumstances you find around you. God will deliver you!" It was as if God were talking directly to me. The words captivated me. I knew they were true, of course, and I always tried to live by them, but it seemed that they were prophetic of something I should prepare myself for. I called Wanice later and told her about it. She also tried to prepare for whatever was in front of me.

A tremendous service followed. Afterwards, Steve, Kristi and I ate lunch together. It felt good to have the original team back together. I had traded my family for Steve's. We were still four Bryants (counting the baby) charging ahead. Kristi updated me as to her condition.

"My doctor has informed me that I am dehydrated, have a rash that could be serious, am anemic, and my blood is too heavy with protein. But most serious is that I still have not gained enough weight. However, the good news is that I no longer have morning sickness!"

We prayed for Kristi and the baby and celebrated the fact that Kristi was no longer sick. Steve drove us back to West Jackson for the second of three speaking engagements for the day. We filled up on the last free gas until Nashville. We drove to West Jackson Baptist church and ate at the church. I met a Mrs. Edmondson. She was 100 years old, yet still teaching Sunday School. She also held Bible studies in her home. She also visited the "youngsters" in nursing homes. For her, anyone under seventy was a youngster.

Just before speaking, we were interviewed by Lisa Young of CBS. After speaking, I met the music minister, Rell Weller. He worked at a Spinal Rehab Center and asked me to come back the next morning to speak. After I left, he made all the arrangements. Steve then drove to Raymond Baptist Church following a carload of deacons from the West Jackson Baptist Church. We arrived fifteen minutes late. The music leader breathed a sigh of relief as we walked in. He was planning on going alphabetically through the hymnal until I arrived. Naturally the congregation was also relieved. I stood to deliver my testimony for the third time in one day. Afterwards we talked in the parking lot with members until 8:30. Steve was just as tired as I was. He drove us back to the West Jackson Baptist Church and hooked us up to the church. Kristi had an unbelievable energy level as she fixed our protein and drinks. She cleaned the RV and planned several days' food preparation. So much for a "day off"!

11

A Mystery Revealed—
Is Our Faith in Mankind or God?

Day 71—Monday, June 11

The last seven weeks of the trip were about to begin. Little did I know that, other than El Capitan, the greatest challenges were still ahead.

Kristi had unbelievable energy as she did all her tasks. She was like a whirlwind. I had not seen this Kristi since the first two weeks of the trip. Rell came by at 8:45, and we followed him to the John H. Webb Rehab Center. I met the patients outside, showed them the RowCycle, and answered their many questions. After testifying about Jesus, I met them personally. Each one had, his own own dreams and goals. I urged them never to give up, regardless of the size of the obstacles.

"I don't know what you are capable of, but what I think is immaterial. You must set your own goals. Then achieve them one by one. God and you must reason together, decide on a direction, then go. If you are not sure what your goals are. Don't just sit still, do something until your goals become apparent to you. Don't ever give up. Each time you give up, quitting becomes easier."

We then drove to the Mississippi Methodist Rehab Center. I was met by CBS, the Jackson newspapers, and other media. We were escorted around the hospital by Isabel White, one of the vice-presidents. I saw every kind of injury and medical treatment imaginable, from an iron lung to a limp. I spoke individually with several patients around the hospital. It was the largest rehab center I had ever seen. At noon, I spoke to a gathering of patients and staff in the lunchroom. We were leaving at 1 when I met Charles. Charles had suffered brain trauma due to a traffic accident. He had severe difficulty in speaking. But he inspired me to continue by saying: "The greatest thing I can do is to glorify God with my body. My body is the temple of God. It does not work as well as it used to, but God can use any 'body' to do great things. I can probably do greater things than most people because I realize that I am weak. So I pray for God's strength. Availability is so much greater than ability."

Steve drove to Carthage to our start point. We arrived at 2:30 in the afternoon. After passing Carthage, we stopped for a break. Frank Taylor stopped his car to talk with us. He was a single-limbed amputee who had seen us pass and eventually caught up with us. Frank was a huge man who weighed 240 pounds. He had only one leg and it was all muscle. His was a recent injury, and he still felt a tremendous loss.

"Frank, I believe you could do this with one arm if you wanted to," I joked.

We laughed and then became serious. I shared my story with him and told him that if Jesus was in his heart, anything was possible. I gave him one of my books and pressed on. We began hitting large hills as we approached Columbus, Mississippi. Kristi drove ahead to the forty-mile mark for the day. She fixed a meal for us under shade trees covered by huge vines. I had been apprehensive about speaking twice that morning because of the impact it would have on our schedule. But because I was obedient in speaking twice we went forty miles without stopping. It was dusk as we drove to Lake Lowndes State Park in Columbus. It was gorgeous! The bugs were chirping and frogs croaking as the moon shone down. Dogs barked in the distance and the stars sparkled diamond-bright.

Coming back from the shower, I glanced down at my feet. The top of my left foot was completely raw. The skin was peeled back and was bleeding. It looked like a bad burn.

"Oh, no, what did I do?" I yelled. Steve and Kristi came running. They doctored it as best they could, but the damage was done. I had no idea how I had hurt my foot or even when. I could feel nothing from the waist down and was constantly hurting myself unknowingly. It could take months for an injury like this to heal. My healing process was slower than most people anyway because of decreased circulation. I was in real trouble. An injury like this could become infected and easily escalate into gangrene. We all prayed for my foot to heal properly. But the big question remained: *How did I do it?* I would not find out how for several days. But there was good news that night. Kristi's baby kicked for the first time.

Day 72—Tuesday, June 12

Early on, Steve heard a loud bang that actually moved the RV a bit. He jumped up, scouted around, and then returned to sleep. Later, we started Day 72 by driving to Columbus Air Force Base and met Gordon and Mike (two DynCorp employees). We learned the loud bang had been an explosion at a nearby chemical plant. Bless the newspersons. They were there. I spoke to the DynCorp employees in several hangars as they worked on T-38 aircraft. I even raced a T-38 down a runway as it taxied. I thought I had him until he took off his brakes and speeded up. Within seconds he was going over 400! Guess what? I lost the race!

During the day, we met a DynCorp employee named Bobby Dupree. He showed us around the entire maintenance facility and offices. We became instant friends. It would become painfully obvious to both of us in less than a week why God had brought us together. He would do more for us than we could possibly anticipate.

We drove to Louisville (Mississippi, pronounced not Louie but Louis) and arrived at 5:30. First Baptist Church graciously lodged us in a hotel.

Day 73—Wednesday, June 13

We decided to take a day off because of three speaking engagements that night and to keep my foot elevated. We rested all day and continued to nurse my foot. It looked even worse the second day, and we prayed that infection would not set in. We ate supper at First Baptist Church; then I shared my testimony. When the service was over, a member of East Louisville Baptist Church gave me a ride to his church while Steve and Kristi loaded the RowCycle and then followed us to the church. I spoke again and then raced to a radio interview. We drove back to First Baptist to hook up the RV. Larry, the janitor, helped.

Day 74—Thursday, June 14

Why have I waited this long to sing, "Row, Row, Row Your Boat"? Rowing again by 7:45, I felt riveted to the RowCycle. Many days and nights I was so tired I wanted to lean back and sleep all night sitting in the

Cycle. This day we had covered thirty-six miles by lunch and resumed again after lunch. It was getting hotter and hillier the further north we went. The Starkville paper came out and talked with us just before a patrolman stopped us. We had been escorted and stopped by several police up to that point so it was just going to be another routine discussion as far as we knew.

"What are you guys doing out here?" he asked sternly.

Steve began explaining it to him so I could save my breath for rowing. Shortly after Steve began, the patrolman cut him off.

"Well, I don't care what you're doing. You're not going to do it on my stretch of road. I want you to stay on the shoulder of the road."

Steve and I looked over at the shoulder. It was *loose gravel.*

"But, Officer, Rob can't ride this on the gravel. It's hard enough on the blacktop. Besides, it is legal for us to be on this road, isn't it? "

"If I say it is unsafe, it becomes illegal. Now get on the shoulder and stay there!" He pulled off before we could open our mouths again.

The gravel was brutal. Each stroke was over 100 pounds, and the gravel was putting nicks in my tires. Steve and I began rolling down a hill, and I began to swerve out of control in the gravel. I almost lost control before moving over into the road long enough to regain my balance.

"Steve, I am going to stay on the road. It is too difficult and dangerous to stay on the shoulder in that thick gravel. Besides, we'll be to Columbus in eight miles and be on a different road."

Steve agreed with me, and we proceeded down the road about a mile before I saw flashing lights in my rearview mirror. The highway patrolman had been watching us and stopped us again.

"Didn't I tell you to stay off the road? I can't believe that you fellows didn't listen to me! If I see you on the road again, I'm not going to give you a ticket. I'll take you to jail!"

"Jail! Are you kidding, Officer?" Steve asked with disbelief. "Officer, if you could just give us an escort to Columbus, we'll be out of your hair," Steve spoke quietly, but with frustration.

"I don't have time to escort you anywhere. Now get over there on that shoulder and stay there. This is your last warning before I take you to jail. I'm going to radio up ahead. You will be watched. If you think I'm tough, just try some areas ahead. Those officers will toss you in jail and throw away the key!"

Steve and I were feeling mighty low, but we followed his commands. We stayed on the shoulder for seven miles, all the way to Columbus. My arms ached and my heart sank, but I prayed that God would intervene. In the 100-degree heat with 90-percent humidity, the work was incredible. I tried not to think about tomorrow. I just concentrated on the job at hand. I knew we could not ride on gravel shoulders across Mississippi and Alabama.

Reporters from the Columbus paper came out, as well as Channel 9, NBC. We were interviewed, and I was tempted to tell them about the police officer. I didn't. I was going to be as obedient to the authorities as I could and let God fight for me. Immediately after the rather lengthy interview with the press, a sheriff I had seen earlier drove by. He, too, was disabled so we had an immediate rapport.

"Sheriff, is it legal for us to be on that highway back there?"

"Sure. Why?"

I told him about the episode with the patrolman. His face turned red. "Did you get a name or badge number?" he screamed.

"No. But even if I did, I wouldn't give it to you. I'm traveling at nine miles an hour, and I have over 1,000 miles to go. I don't want to start a war with the police. I'll lose."

Bobby Dupree showed up to cheer us on. I also shared the incident with him. Between his phone calls and the sheriff's radio, within five minutes, we had an escort from a county deputy and a city policeman all the way to the border of Alabama.

Don't tell me that God can't fight our battles for us better than we can ourselves! I thought.

To go as quickly as possible for the sake of the two lawmen who were with us, I rowed another five miles at eleven miles an hour (two miles per hour faster than my average). We finished at fifty-two miles for the day. I took off my shirt and actually wrung water out of it. We drove back to Lowndes Lake State Park. The mystery of my raw foot was about to be solved.

I took a shower in the same stall I had been in before. Leaning forward to wash my hair, I felt a burn behind my left ear. I leaned back and looked up at the hot water handle. Trickling down from behind the handle was scalding hot water. My eyes followed the dripping water down to my left foot. It was directly under the scalding hot water again. It was burned even worse now. It was an open sore, and blood ran out of my foot. Now it was a first-degree burn! It looked more like hamburger than a foot. I immediately pulled my leg back and washed as quickly as I could. I dressed the foot in bandages again. We prayed it would not get infected. But the devil was not through with me. Another severe challenge was right around the corner.

Day 75—Friday, June 15

Kristi was a whirlwind of energy. While Steve and I entered Alabama, Kristi went to the store, bank, post office, made phone calls, and did all the laundry. She was doing everything on her list just as the other drivers had done.

On a particularly tough hill, Steve and I were praying for strength and endurance in the heat and humidity. It was only 10 in the morning, and it was already approaching 100 degrees. Suddenly a car pulled over, and a family, the Bill Edons, jumped out, calling Steve by name. They were friends of Steve's from Florida. I don't believe it was a coincidence. I sort of believe the Lord sent them along to pat Steve on the back. As a matter of fact, they were wondering how the "Row Across America" was going. We prayed together for a minute before I pressed on and left Steve to talk with them. The terrain we had traveled across our nation reminded me of a shaky corporation's sales figures or a see-saw's up and down, up and down. But at least a thousand times I thanked the Lord that we didn't have to spend all of our time on flat, monotonous ground or on hilly or mountainous levels, either. Isn't it marvelous how God grants us variety?

The hills loomed larger and steeper as we approached Tuscaloosa. I even had to push on the wheels a few times. We were rowing again by 1. Steve had not caught up with me yet when the Gordo chief of police stopped me.

Oh no! Are we going to jail? Has that officer radioed ahead to the Alabama Police? I wondered. *This is great! I'm going to jail, and Steve is not even here,* I thought. I held my breath as he walked over to me. He stuck out his hand, smiled, and introduced himself.

"How about an escort through my town? I heard you were coming. I'm glad I saw you. Can I have your autograph?"

He gave me an escort through Gordo as Steve caught up with me. The officer "back there" had told us that the police ahead were even worse. He could not have been more mistaken. The police helped us all the way across the state, even in the middle of the night.

After he left we had two hair-raising close calls with a car and a logging truck. The woods were extra thick this time of the year. It seemed that every other truck was a logger. Lumber mills were everywhere. We passed several furniture manufacturers.

Steve and I were drinking over a quart of water per hour each. This kept Steve busy stopping to refill our supply. We drank four quarts of water apiece that afternoon alone. We stopped for the day at the bottom of a large hill with forty-two more miles behind us. The air was heavy with humidity. We drove to Lake Lurleen State Park deep in the hills of Tuscaloosa. While I was taking a shower, the rain poured downhard, and I was trapped in the rest-room with an oil-field hand named Raymond. Knowing that this was no coincidence I shared my testimony with him, and we talked about similar experiences we had had in the oil fields. Steve helped me back to the RV, and we stayed in woods high above the beautiful lake.

Day 76—Saturday, June 16

At 8 we began our climb into Tuscaloosa up several large hills. There was no shoulder, and Steve had another close call with a logging truck. Kristi informed us that the media would not be available until Monday, and I had a nagging feeling that I was supposed to stop for the day. But it was only 10. I hated to waste that much daylight, but I was obedient to that still small Voice in my heart. That Voice had not let us down yet! We stopped at the Northport Mall. We went only ten miles, but it was a blessing we did. God had already begun to orchestrate a logistic miracle involving three men from California, a pastor there in Tuscaloosa, and a friend back home in Texas.

We drove over 100 miles to Moulton, Alabama, where I spoke at a youth rally. I was so overcome with emotion that I could not finish speaking. I was not sure why I was so upset, but it could have been the Spirit within me who knew what was going to happen within forty-eight hours. While I signed books, several of the youth and leadership told me that I had spoken directly to them, and that they were the reason I had come. Despite the fact that I was not able to finish, God had spoken mightily to the people that night. As a matter of fact, one of the youth there would run into me in a seeming coincidence and uplift me the following week when I needed it.

Steve drove us back to Shiloh Baptist Church in Tuscaloosa. We arrived at 1 AM completely out of gas. We hooked up to the church. Steve looked out of the window and said, "Well, at least the neighbors won't bother us!" We had parked next to a huge cemetery.

Day 77—Sunday, June 17

We ate breakfast at the pastor's home next door. His name was David Allen. We all became friends immediately. I had no idea what a grand part in the "Row Across America" he was about to play. I spoke to Shiloh Baptist Church and then ate lunch with the congregation. They gave us a love offering and sent us on our way. David followed us to a gas station, then Steve drove us 120 miles back to Ackerman, Mississippi. It began raining and continued all day. Kristi doctored my foot en route. It looked horrible! We met the pastor, Rob Faulk, and stayed at his house until the service. The youth sang several songs that could melt the wax in your ears. Their church was growing and doing well. We were immediately endeared to each other. The church gave us a love offering and prayed for us to finish, especially praying for my burned foot. After the service we stayed with J. T. and Imogene Perry. They were a wonderful older couple who took us in, fed us, and loved us like their own kids. The pastor and pastor's wife came and gave Kristi a baby gift. Imogene loaded us down with fresh vegetables from her garden and pounds of food to take with us. Even though I am not a pastor, they virtually gave us an old-fashioned (what they used to call) "pounding." The Spirit within her anticipated we would need the food rather soon.

Day 78—Monday, June 18

Imogene fixed breakfast at 5:30 AM, and we were "on the road again" by 6:30. Steve drove us clear to Tuscaloosa. He was exhausted after all the weekend driving.

We started again at 10 AM after speaking with two network television stations. We received an escort by three motorcycle policemen. They were incredible. They had it down to a science. As a matter of fact, we built a rapport with them that we would need early the next morning. God had just put the last piece together for a support group that spanned the country!

We passed through Tuscaloosa. The road was so bad grass was growing up through the seams of the pavement. It pounded on the axles. I prayed my axles would not break like they had in the desert.

Just before we were to eat lunch, Kristi smiled at both of us, turned the RV around, and drove back to Tuscaloosa. *Why?* I wondered.

"Steve, where is she going?" I asked.

"She just has a few errands to run," he replied quietly.

We continued the rest of the morning and into the early afternoon. Steve bought some Gatorade and we pressed on. Steve was always quiet, but when he didn't talk at all, I could tell there was a problem. We were almost to Birmingham. On a break I asked one more time, "Where is Kristi?"

Steve looked down toward the ground with a tear in his eye. He fought back his emotions, and bit his lip.

He was absolutely overcome and said, "This morning, when she woke up, she was bleeding, and there was water all over the bed. She's gone to the doctor to see if she's losing the baby."

That rocked me back on my heels. It seemed as though our worst fears might become tragic realities. My eyes teared up and I prayed, "No, Lord. No!"

Both of us wept as we continued as quickly as possible to a phone to call the hospital. Kristi had already left the hospital. We exited Highway 11 and proceeded north on the interstate. Within half an hour, Kristi returned in tears. The doctor indicated her body was trying to cause a miscarriage. In his opinion, to save the baby she must go home, see her doctor, and stay in bed.

We stopped at mile marker 100 and drove to Tannehill State Park. Steve bought a ticket for Kristi to fly home the following morning. In the meantime, I also called Wanice.

Wanice was understandably upset. She had not planned on leaving home until our arrival in Washington. This meant she was going to have to drop everything and come running. After a brief discussion, we planned for Steve and me to go ahead alone until Wanice arrived a week later. I was on my way back to the RV to tell them about Kristi's ticket and Wanice's plan to join us. Steve met me on the trail. He was completely broken when he confessed, "Rob, I want to go home, too."

I whirled around and faced him, "You do?"

"Yes. Kristi needs me."

I knew he was right. His first responsibility was to his own family. But this meant I would be stranded at the RV park for a week waiting for Wanice to arrive. I had food and water, but this would throw off all of the speaking engagements. I did not want to let Steve go! He was security for me. Everytime I was in trouble thus far, Steve had been there.

But that still small Voice in my heart said, "Let him go. Do you trust in mankind or in Me?"

Steve then bought a ticket for himself, too. I called my friend Bobby Dupree, my fellow employee at Columbus Air Force Base, to see if he could take Steve and Kristi to the airport the next morning. He did one better. Because of the friendship we had developed with the Tuscaloosa police, he arranged a police escort for Steve and Kristi all the way to the Birmingham International Airport.

I called Wanice back and told her I was going to be stranded, and she began to cry.

"Wanice, I've been telling churches all across America that if God is for us, there is no power that can stop us. Well, it's time to see what we really believe." She agreed with me and called as many friends as she could to begin praying. Prayers were being said coast to coast from friends and relatives. I was about to watch God go to work. I took a bath in a real bathtub in the park restroom. It was the only easy bath I had taken since leaving California. I realized that I had not eaten since breakfast over sixteen hours ago. After the bath, Steve fixed a bite to eat.

I called Wanice back at midnight to tell her good-night and not to worry. When she answered she was crying again. But this time it was tears of joy.

"Rob, you're not going to believe this. Don Bright lost his job two weeks ago, and God promised him the reason would be revealed right away. As soon as I called, God verified in his heart that this was it. He'll be there in two weeks and ride the rest of the way to Washington with you. I'm also coming in two weeks. We'll meet you in Nashville. Gary Leroy just happens to be flying to Nashville in two weeks, and he's going to drive the car back! Also, Bob Peterson is flying in for the last week before Washington to help me."

"But Wanice, what about the next two weeks? How do I get to Nashville. I can't row two weeks all by myself."

"Rob!" she paused and began crying again.

"Jeff is coming tomorrow. He's giving up another two weeks of vacation for you. He'll be there tomorrow at 5 PM. Rob, two weeks ago, Jeff felt he was supposed to cancel these next two weeks of meetings and traveling. He didn't know why until I called. God told him four words, 'Take care of them.' He's leaving so fast he'll have to tell his boss why later."

I began crying with Wanice. It was tears of sadness for Steve and Kristi and tears of unworthiness of friendships like Jeff and Don. Suddenly the mystery of why Jeff had to be on the first two weeks of the trip was revealed. He was the only man who understood how the RV worked and knew the routine well enough to respond in such an emergency. God had begun working two weeks before and, with the help of Wanice and friends, put it all together in four hours. I was in bed at 12:30 AM. Steve, Kristi, and I were emotionally and physically exhausted.

I didn't know what to say to Steve and Kristi to ease their pain. I wrestled with guilt that I had pushed Kristi too hard in her condition. I prayed that God's grace would be sufficient for them to stand the testing ahead of them. Next to God, of course, the most important thing in Steve's life was his family, but I recognized he was devastated that he could not finish the trip. He had ridden his bike 2,200 miles at my side. Now the trip for Steve was over. Or was it?

12

The Relentless Hills—
Trials Strengthen Our Faith!

Day 79—Tuesday, June 19

Steve woke me at 4 AM to tell me good-bye. Again, I was looking into the eyes of my thirteen-year-old brother. It was almost as if we were transported back in time to our childhood. I was eighteen and heading off into the "wild blue yonder" of the Air Force. Steve and I had always been close. We depended on each other daily after our parents' divorce. We were always there for each other, But now I had to leave. I said it through tears. It was harder for me than it was for Steve. I was the one doing the abandoning.

Steve tried to ease my conscience by saying, "Rob, you don't have a choice. You have to go. I'll be OK." Even so, Steve did not learn until much later that I carried the guilt of that moment with me every day of my life.

Suddenly, I was back in the present. Except now the roles were reversed. This time he had to leave me. All the facade was stripped away as we looked into each other's eyes. Steve could only say, "I'm sorry."

This time, it was my turn to ease his mind. I repeated what he had told me seventeen years before. "Steve, you don't have a choice. You have to go. I'll be OK."

He stood there split between his family and leaving his paraplegic brother alone. Sensing his pain, I said, "Steve, I'm sorry for putting you in this position, but you don't have a choice. "

I begged Steve to let me pay for his tickets. As much as the trip had cost me, I had not left my job like Steve had. He would not take my credit card. He turned and walked back out to Kristi. She left without a word. I could not imagine the trauma she was experiencing.

The police were waiting for them. I watched the car go out of sight. They were gone, and the RV was quiet and lonely. Everything I looked at reminded me of Steve and Kristi's sacrifice. I decided I was going to finish for all four of us—the baby, too! Nothing was going to stop me short of death! I never fell deeply asleep. I slept only three-and-a-half hours.

Is Kristi going to lose the baby? Is it your fault?

I also felt guilty for thinking of myself. *How are you going to row forty miles today? How are you going to get to the airport later today to pick up Jeff? You can't drive the RV. It does not have hand controls.*

Rising at 6:00, I crawled outside to my wheelchair and went to the phone. The only person I could think to call was David Allen, the pastor of Shiloh Baptist Church. I called and David answered. "Brother, I'll be there in one hour," he answered instantly.

Meanwhile, the Elmores in the neighboring RV came over, and we talked. It helped me pass the time. I drank two cups of coffee with them struggling to stay awake.

Sure enough, David arrived one hour later and even brought Jay Cork, a young man who rode Steve's bike with me. We began at 9 AM using State Highway 20.

Jay rode the bike with me and David drove the RV. The air was heavy with emotions as we continued hour after hour. I guess God knew I needed a good laugh. One was a few moments away.

I was struggling up a hill, moving at about six miles per hour, sweat pouring down my face. A long, fancy Cadillac pulled up beside me. A man leaned over toward me.

"Where are you going?" he asked.

"I'm going from Los Angeles to Washington, D.C."

He stared at me for a minute then asked, "Today?"

I looked at him laughing, thinking he was kidding. But he was serious. This made me laugh even harder. He probably thought I was incredibly rude, but I could not stop laughing. Jay was laughing, too.

The man was still waiting for an answer.

"No, it's going to take almost a whole week!"

Satisfied, he pulled away. Jay and I laughed the rest of the morning.

Right outside of Birmingham, David and Jay went ahead to call the media. While they were gone, Neil came along on a bike. He was the meanest-looking bike-rider I had ever seen. He smiled at me but seemed to glare at everyone else.

"You're in a rough neighborhood, my friend. Just stick with me. I ride here all the time. They won't mess with you as long as you're with me."

After looking around, I didn't question him. He was a man of few words, reminding me of Steve. He disappeared shortly before the RV returned. I wondered if he had wings tucked under his shirt. We received a police escort by Officer Gary G. Finley all the way through Birmingham. I talked the hours away with Officer Finley as we passed over the large hills surrounding the city. It was over 100 degrees by lunch. He took us all the way to Fultondale where we were met by Officer C. E. Reedy of the Fultondale police. We were also escorted by the Gardendale and Mount Olive police departments. Slowly the miles went by. I continued to pray for Steve and Kristi all day. We finished for the day at exactly forty miles, and David and Jay dropped me off at the airport. We were richer for having known one another.

The plane was late. I called Steve and Kristi. They were not sure what would happen with the baby, but I continued to call them every day for a week.

Finally, Jeff's plane landed. I fought back the nagging feeling that he had missed his plane and that now I was stranded at the airport. I waited until the last wave of people walked out. There he was! Over dinner, we talked about how two people were going to do the job of three. While we talked, I realized that twenty-four hours before, I was uncertain whether the trip could keep on going, yet here I was with Jeff. My body was much tireder, yet my faith was ten times stronger.

Day 80—Wednesday, June 20

Finally, a day off! Still, I had two in-studio television interviews in the morning and a church speaking appointment that night. We drove to the top of the tallest hill in Birmingham to a taped interview with Channel 6, ABC. Jeff and I took our time unloading the RowCycle. We were led into the studio. I was asked to sit beside the co-host who had a cast on his leg.

"What's this, the handicapped section?" I asked with a smile.

"No, I broke my leg skydiving," he answered, laughing. He then talked into the camera.

I had been told that we would be taped, but we were going on live. I barely finished tying my tie when the cameras turned to me. We talked for over ten minutes about our trip and my faith. The only reason he had picked up my book was because of his own temporary handicap. He gave the book rave reviews.

Jeff and I then drove to Florence, Alabama, over four hours away. We went to the NBC station for the second interview. Afterwards, I was informed that a basketball coach from Samford University had seen the interview in Birmingham and wanted me to speak to his team the next day. I agreed to come. Jeff almost fainted! We already had nineteen speaking engagements in the next thirteen days, and I just agreed to another. But after thinking about it, that was what the trip was all about. Immediately after we drove to Underwood Baptist Church in Florence.

Pastor Donnie McDaniel hosted us at supper (dinner in the north). We raced back to the service in the nick of time. I was exhausted over the events of the past several days, and I prayed for God's strength. The church gave us a love offering, and I later found out that the Baptist director of missions for that area had been in the service. Pastor McDaniel told me later that the director of missions said he would rather have been in that service than a week-long revival meeting. That did boost our spirits!

Jeff drove us back to Birmingham in a spectacular lightning storm. It was 90 degrees with 90-percent humidity at 10 PM! Jeff was doing the work of both Steve and Kristi, so I suppose he was worn out as I was. We were in bed at 1 AM. So much for another day off!

Day 81—Thursday, June 21

We were met by the police at the start point. Jeff and I unloaded the RowCycle. Jeff had a recurring back problem, so I prayed for Jeff's back. If it went out, we would both be in deep trouble. I also prayed for the RV and RowCycle. With a two-man team, we could not afford to have breakdowns. Now that Steve was gone, I was alone on the road. There was no one to talk to. When the RowCycle broke down, I had to fix it myself. I was carrying ten pounds of tools, extra springs, and paraphernalia to fix the RowCycle. I could feel the extra weight. Also, Jeff could never venture too far out of radio range. I had to let him know when I was out of water or having other problems.

Media coverage around Birmingham had been so heavy that hundreds of cars and trucks were honking their horns, and the drivers stopped or waved. This helped my loneliness and sadness concerning Steve, Kristi, and the baby.

Soon, I was met by Officer Ralph Holliyam of the Morris police and after that by a deputy sheriff of Jefferson County. When the road ended at the interstate, I told the officer I was going to use the interstate.

"That's not legal, but there's no other safe route. So, I didn't hear you say that. But, unofficially, I agree with you."

My mind wandered back to the Mississippi policeman who threatened to throw us in jail and warned us about the Alabama police. We certainly found out he was seriously wrong. I also recognized he did not represent the typical Mississippi lawman, either. No doubt many of them would have been embarrassed by his actions.

Soon after, it began to rain. The clouds were dark and ominous. A car stopped, and a young lady jumped out.

"I saw you as I passed going the opposite way. You've got to get out of here. You're not going to believe the storm I just passed through. It was raining so hard that traffic was slowed to twenty miles an hour. A man has been hit and killed by lightning, and the flooding is terrible. In addition, tornadoes have been sighted. You've got to get out of here."

I thanked her for her concern, but I was behind schedule. Besides, I had a speaking engagement in the afternoon that was going to cut the day short anyway. I pressed on.

Lightning began to strike everywhere, and the wind began to buffet me. Soon the wind was so strong I could not even hear Jeff on the radio. Then the storm accelerated to almost tornadic force. I was virtually drowning. It was raining so hard I was blinded, and I prayed that the slow-moving traffic could see me. I hit a very steep hill over two miles long. Water rushed down the hill against me. But I was not going to quit. I had to finish for Steve, Kristi, and the baby.

Suddenly a van pulled over, and a man jumped out with a camera. He was from the NBC from Birmingham. The cameraman videotaped me and just shook his head. I talked with him briefly. He could not believe that I was out in the storm. It was so dark that he could barely see me as I began again. I asked him to watch me as I crossed an exit ramp. He told me that it was clear as far as he could see. He was still running his camera as I crossed the ramp against the wind and rain. Just then a truck zoomed by up the ramp. My heart almost stopped. Soon the storm passed, and I continued to row until 12:30. We loaded everything up and drove back to Samford University in Birmingham. I met Coach McClain, and he introduced me to the kids in a summer training camp. They were ages eight through eighteeen. I said: "Never give up on your dreams of excellence, both physically and academically. If you are going to finish what you start, you are going to have to pay the price. In order to accomplish your dreams, there will be pain and the forfeiture of time and energy. Is it worth it? Only you can answer that question. Both success and failure are learned traits. Which trait are you going to begin developing? You are young, strong, and smart. Begin a winning attitude now; what you can accomplish with faith in God and the right attitude is up to you."

It continued to rain all night. Jeff and I stayed in the RV and waited out the storm. The wind howled like a banshee. We took the time to finish organizing the RV for a two-man team. Sometime during the night, the rain stopped.

Day 82—Friday, June 22

Jeff and I unloaded the RowCycle together, and I was row, row, rowing by 7:50. After a mile-long hill, I left the interstate and passed through Cullman. I was met by Officer Frances Styles. When it began to rain again, she spoke to me more like a mother than an officer and asked me if I wanted to stop. I sneezed once, and she gave me a maternal lecture on taking care of myself. It felt good to know she cared. I felt like giving her a hug. After what we had been through, I needed a hug myself, but I fought the urge. Several people clapped outside a restaurant as we passed. We stopped at a car dealership for a break, and the Cullman reporters came out. Both Frances and the salesmen who worked at the dealership had a warning for me. "Get on the interstate. Don't take Highway 31. There's a hill there even cars and trucks have difficulty getting over."

I had told Jeff we were going to access the interstate because of the hills up ahead. However, it began to rain again, and I opted to stay on Route 31. The episode with the truck on the ramp had scared me, I readily admit. Jeff drove by, and I tried to tell him to come back, but he could not hear me because of the rain. Officer Styles and I began again. I knew that when Jeff did not find me on the interstate that he would double back. I thought of the time we had been separated in Palm Springs on the other side of the country. This time, Jeff did not panic. He simply called the police and received my location from the dispatcher.

He joined us just as I went down "the hill." They had not misled me. It was the steepest hill of the trip. It was not as long as the mountains I had been over, but it was steeper. It seemed to go straight down and straight up. I reached a speed of forty miles an hour downhill. The Row-Cycle was very unstable at that speed, but I wanted to see if I could reach forty. The trip uphill was not as much fun, of course. My speed was about one mile per hour. I would pull on the handles until my arms felt as if they were being torn from my torso. I repeated this torture until I topped the hill. Jeff cheered me on.

We thought we had it whipped until we came to Brindley Mountain outside Hartselle. It was a small but steep mountain. I had my brakes on, but with the water from the road and oil on my wheels, I was still moving downhill at thirty-three miles an hour. I began to swerve out of control and barely kept from overturning before reaching the bottom. I was going to have to change my brakes now that I was in the Appalachians. When Don Bright came, this problem was fixed.

We ate lunch at the "Coral," and I made calls to the press and the next several pastors. Then I met two splendid pastors from separate churches—Mickey Brackin and Thomas Smothers. They were helpful in calling the press and taking care of us while we were in the area.

We somehow made it through the next string of mountains and finished at forty-two miles outside Decatur. We met the press there.

Words can't describe the loveliness of Point Mallard State Park. The tree-covered hills were so green and plush we almost decided to stay there and forget the trip. As I barbecued chicken, Jeff and I watched the sun go down behind the hills. The deep red and orange colors produced a myriad of hues. It was awe-inspiring. We wished our wives were there to share the moment.

We took a breath before having thirteen speaking engagements in the next nine days.

Day 83—Saturday, June 23

Channel 12, CBS, and the Huntsville and Decatur papers met us at the start point. Soon our police escort arrived, and we were rowing by 9:15. We passed through Decatur and across the Tennessee River Bridge. The river was glistening, and we were thankful for the police escort across the narrow bridge. Then I was reminded of the chant we did as children, "Rain, rain, go away! Come again another day." Yep. It started raining again. But there was just a slight head wind, and the hills were small. Soon we passed a huge guided missile that marked the Alabama Welcome Center. Just before moving into Tennessee, I was stopped by a young man. I noticed that he was using hand controls on his car just as I do.

"I'm a quadriplegic. I can't use my arms like you can, but you have inspired me never to quit. I've read about you and have wanted to meet you. Please don't give up. To me, you represent the undaunted spirit that all of us as Americans should possess. I'll never throw in the towel again. Finish for all us who can't!"

Soon after, we passed the Tennessee state line. I told my aching body that we had just about 1,000 miles to go. The young quadriplegic inspired me to push myself harder. We stopped a mile later at forty-two for the day. We drove back fifty miles to the First Baptist Church of Arab, Alabama. We met Pastor Allan Ragley, his wife Gloria, and their children. We ate pounds of lasagna, a weakness I have in common with Garfield, the fat cat of the cartoons.

Two other churches also came to the service. The crowd was predominantly kids, and God moved on their hearts. Then it was back to Birmingham and to sleep in a hotel, compliments of Trussville Southside Baptist Church.

Day 84—Sunday, June 24

We arrived at Trussville Southside at 10. Several deacons helped Jeff carry the RowCycle inside. The walls of the sanctuary were covered with beautifully stained knotty pine. After the service, we ate with Pastor Ronnie and his wife Beverly.

Jeff and I raced seventy miles to Concord Baptist Church in Cullman. I had been waiting for this church for over 2,300 miles. I would never forget the call several months before from the pastor asking us to come.

"Rob, this is the pastor of Concord Baptist Church. I'm not going to mislead you. This is a very small church, but you just have to come."

"Pastor, I'm sorry, but I'm already booked in your area."

"Rob, you *have* to come. The chairman of our deacon body, Bud Hanes, has been hurt in a farming accident. He's a paraplegic now, and our church is broken-hearted over it. Rob, you *must* come."

"Yes, you're right. I believe I do have to be there."

Upon hanging up, I cancelled a large church in order to speak at Concord Baptist.

Concord was over 100 years old, a small rural church surrounded by pastures and cattle, with a cemetery nearby. There was an old cross in front of the building that looked as ancient as the century-old brick. I met Bud Hanes, the deacon who had joined the ranks of us paraplegics. As he fought back the tears, he testified he had been told by well-meaning believers that "if he had any faith, he'd be walking." I delivered a sermon along with my testimony about true faith. Part of my message dealt with the apostle Paul.

"Who are we to dictate to God who He should heal and who He shouldn't? Paul prayed three times to be healed and God said no. Somehow I believe that Paul had enough faith for anything to come to pass, if all it takes is to tell God what He should and should not do. The true prayer of faith is one that seeks God's mind and then prays for the thing that God places in the heart."

There was not a dry eye in the packed church building. Bud's entire family was there. It was a time of healing, perhaps not physical but emotional and spiritual. God honored my obedience by going to that small church. We sold more books there than we had in churches three times its size. The church also gave us a generous love offering before sending us on our way.

Jeff drove us thirty miles to the next church. The pastor was not sure if he wanted me to follow through with a message. Finally, he shrugged his shoulders and said that it couldn't hurt. I thought his attitude strange, but I then gave my testimony. I said things I had never said before. I spoke of God's authority and seeking His mind before making important decisions in our lives and in our churches. I thought that I had totally missed it, but when I gave the invitation, half the church came forward. The pastor didn't tell me why until after the service. The church deacons had just voted for him to vacate the pastorate. The church and he were severely wounded. I did not know if my sermon changed the outcome, but I was sure that I had presented what God had wanted.

We drove three hours back to the Tennessee state line and stayed on the side of the road.

Day 85—Monday, June 25

Shortly after beginning at 7:30, I was going up a hill and approaching a bridge. There was a car parked on the side of the road. As I passed it, a lady stepped out and yelled two words, "Home coming!"

I wondered what type of word association game we were playing, so I hollered back, "Football game, pom-poms, cheerleaders . . ."

"No! Home coming."

I thought this person needed psychiatric care so I started again. I was halfway across the bridge moving uphill at a turtle's pace, when she screamed at me this time, *"Home coming!"*

I turned to look at her in wonder. Then I saw it. Right behind, barreling toward me, was a house (home) being moved on a huge tractor-trailer. I grabbed the handles and thought I would break them off trying to row to the other side. I moved over just as the truck passed. I waved back at the lady, and she waved back. From now on when playing charades and someone says "home coming," my word association is going to be, "Bridge, lady, pain, tractor-trailer, and 'Look behind you.' "

It was the first dry day in over a week. I was ready to row despite three speaking engagements on the previous day. The birds were singing; the rain was finally over. I realized for the first time on the trip that the RowCycle had gone eight days without a breakdown. God was taking care of it in Steve's absence.

The newspapers came out in Pulaski. I was so busy singing with the birds I had rowed thirty miles by 1:30. It was already over 90 degrees, and the humidity was climbing. The hills were smaller but they were relentless. There was no flat ground. After lunch I was crawling back into the RowCycle as two old men watched. I recloned they were lazily sitting there talking about bygone days. I envied them for their peaceful, slow ways.

I was ready to begin when one of them said, "If I was disabled, I would be driving a car, not that thing. That looks like too much work to me, Son. How far are you going?"

"From coast to coast, over 3,000 miles."

He simply stood there with a look of disbelief.

"Well, Son, good luck. I'll sit here in the shade and drink my tea. I admire you. I wished I had done something like that when I was young."

I began rowing again and thought about his words. I wondered how many people just sit under the shade tree of life and watch their dreams go by until it's too late to do anything about them. Is it ever too late?

We passed through Columbia and the local press came out. Thinking about the old man's words, I just could not stop rowing. I finally stopped in total exhaustion at over fifty-five miles! I talked to Wanice that night. She had scheduled two more speaking engagements. Jeff and I shuffled our speaking schedule to fit them in.

We sat out in the twilight eating watermelon and talking. We didn't talk about the trip, just about our families and jobs. Afterward, we turned in for the night. Before fading off to sleep, I looked over at Jeff. If he had not come a week ago, the trip could have been over. I didn't have to explain what I was thinking. I simply said, "Thanks, Jeff."

"You're welcome, Rob! But when God says 'Take care of them,' I would be out of God's will in not coming."

I marveled at his faith and attitude. Judy had been told for the first time, "Take care of them," eight years before when I had fallen from the oil derrick. They visited me in the hospital without fail and took care of my family until I could. That "take care of them" had spanned eight years now. I was so thankful for friends like Jeff and Judy Wilson.

Day 86—Tuesday, June 26

At 7:30 it was so cool we could see our breath. The hills were relentless again. My hands and arms were numb. We passed through Franklin and Brentwood before receiving a police escort into Nashville. We arrived too early for a scheduled appearance at the Baptist Sunday School Board so I talked with Officer Joe alongside the road. He had lost his teenage daughter a year before. I listened. I had no words for him. I just listened. It seemed to help him knowing that he was talking to someone who had also suffered.

At 2, I rowed to the Baptist Sunday School Board and was met by about 100 people. I saw several old friends. Nashville media folk came, and I spoke briefly with them.

Jeff and I drove all the way back past Decatur, Alabama, to the Somerville area to New Friendship Baptist Church. I was lying there resting before going to the service, when I turned to Jeff.

"I somehow think Steve needs to talk with me."

"Why is that?" Jeff asked.

"I sometimes know when something really bad is wrong with him. When an old girl friend broke up with him, I knew something was wrong and went to his house. I was there for him. We have always had an unusual relationship. We have been as close as two brothers can be. I hope it's not trouble with the baby!"

At 7, I spoke to the congregation. There had been a death in the church a few days before: a young deacon. The church was suffering, and I spoke on sorrow and our reaction to it.

Jeff and I went to a hotel compliments of Mickey Brackin's and Thomas Smothers's churches. Jeff called home. Then he walked into my room with an expression of surprise.

"Rob, you need to call home. You were right—Steve does need to talk with you. He has called one of our friends in California asking if some airline tickets could be refunded. He was told they were non-refundable, but he wants you to call him anyway."

I called Steve and he answered.

"Steve, how is Kristi? Is she OK?"

"Yes, everything here is fine. Rob, I want to come back!"

I could not believe it. Even if there was a one-percent chance of losing the baby, how could he take the risk and come back? He said the doctor thought there was no problem and that Kristi's water had not broken like it had appeared. Steve said that with rest, she would be in tip-top shape. I remembered when they told me on the second day of the trip the pregnancy would not be a problem. Yet, five weeks later Kristi went home for a month. Then, just eight days after her return, I was left stranded at an RV park. I was not prepared to chance it again. I answered no! I gave him three reasons:

1. Kristi needed him more than I did.
2. If he came, Don would go home, and I could be stranded again if Kristi needed him.
3. Most importantly, if Kristi lost the baby and Steve was with me instead of her, I would never forgive myself.

Steve disagreed strongly with me and said that it was his decision, not mine. I knew how much I was hurting him. I wanted Steve there so badly I could hardly stand it, but I had no other decision that I could live with. In addition, I saw firsthand how God had worked out replacing Steve before we even knew a problem existed. Once again I said no.

Day 87—Wednesday, June 27

I did not sleep at all that night because of my conversation with Steve. I was sure that he and Kristi were hurting, too. I felt that I had made the right decision, but I still felt terrible. I was plagued all night with doubt and depression. I lay there with a badly burned foot, a sprained ankle, my hands so numb I could not even make a fist. I was tired, my weight was down, I had no energy left, and I had suffered heavy financial losses.

Jeff and I went in to a local eatery for a place to hide. I was totally beaten. I was prepared to call the whole thing off and go back to the comfort of my home and family. Just then a young woman served us. She looked at me strangely.

"You spoke at a youth rally a week ago in Moulton, Alabama. I was there. There were so many of us who were so discouraged with life's problems until you came. You cut right to the heart of what's important. You said that we have a cross to bear, but that it is nothing compared to what Christ has done for us. Now when I look at my problems, they fade into nothing compared to Jesus hanging on that cross for me. Christ died so we could be free from sin and be given His strength to meet life's challenges. In Christ, all things are possible, you said. You told us the story of how David faced Goliath, knowing that if God gives us a dream, then there is no power that can stop us. Thanks for coming to my church. I've been praying that nothing stops you and that you can tell all those other churches what you told us!"

She walked away. She had given me back the exact words I had given her. But I had not been listening to my heart. I had been looking at the problem, not the Problem Solver. Suddenly in my mind's eye, I saw the demon standing in the middle of the road trying to stop me again. But the angels were bigger and stronger and pulled on the handles until he disappeared. I had almost fallen for the devil's deceptions again. Depression is one of his most powerful weapons!

I walked back out of that Dairy Queen a new man. That young woman will never know that she had changed the outcome of the trip, and possibly my life.

That night I spoke at a local Baptist church. They had advertised that I was coming, and the church was filled! I stood to speak, and there was a standing ovation, the first one ever before I spoke. I think everyone there felt excitement and anticipation for what God was about to say through me. Jeff told me later that although he had heard me over and over, each time it was a little different. I could not believe the powerful words that were coming out of my mouth. God was there! After I finished there was a moment of silence, then another standing ovation. But this time, they were clapping for God!

After the service, a man handed us a one-hundred-dollar bill for a single book. It was the largest number of books sold on the trip so far.

We drove back to the Baptist Sunday School Board in Nashville and slept in the parking lot.

13

There's No Mountain Too Tall—
We Teach Success or Failure to Our Children by Example

Day 88—Thursday, June 28

We were rowing by 9. Officer Joe came back and escorted us again while Jeff went off to do his jobs for the day. We went through the heavy rush-hour traffic of downtown Nashville. He told me on his intercom where to turn. He would blare his siren in the intersections. His bright lights flashed constantly. He was enjoying escorting me as much I enjoyed the escort. We stopped at an intersection and a young lady waved at me to get my attention. I looked at her and she motioned behind me.

"Hey, there's a policeman behind you, I think he wants you to pull over." I told her thank you but I knew he was there. Joe was laughing out loud.

Soon we were on Highway 31-East. Jeff caught up at 10:30 in Hendersonville. We were escorted by Keith Hill, a motorcycle policeman. There were a lot of people waving all day because of media coverage.

We received another police escort through Gallatin and stopped at 2 for the day. We drove back to Nashville and checked into a hotel compliments of Broadman Press. Wanice finally arrived and met us at the hotel. Wanice put all her stuff into the RV as Jeff and I drove to Lebanon and spoke to another Baptist church. Wanice was a welcome sight, along with the boys.

We were all asleep by midnight. I was quite excited about speaking at the Baptist Sunday School Board chapel service the following morning. The Board is the largest publisher of religious materials in the world.

Day 89—Friday, June 29

After an early breakfast came chapel at 7:30. For one of the first times on the trip, I was nervous. After all, what could I possibly say to all of those "Doctors?" I spoke for eighteeen minutes. What followed was a standing ovation. I pray it was for our Lord and not for me. That's how it ought to be.

As I shook hands, one person remarked to another, "He's coming to my little country church."

As a matter of fact, I was asked to cancel a smaller church, already scheduled, for a huge church. No was my answer. It was tough, but I believed God would honor my decision.

I signed books from 9 to 10 AM at the Board cafeteria and then went to the Baptist Book Store for another autograph party. I even received a proclamation from the mayor of Nashville. I went to Channel 66 for an interview and then two more radio stations. Frances Meeker, religion editor of the *Nashville Banner*, was thorough with her coverage. after returning to my family, I rode a trolley car around Nashville with my boys. That's when I met Stanley from Czechoslovakia. His country had just overthrown its communist government. He rejoiced at the giant sky-scrapers and affluence of America.

"I'm free to be anything I want now. My country will be like this someday. My homeland will die before returning to communism."

Tearfully, he continued, "America is so great. I have wanted to see it all my life. It stands as a shining example to the world what freedom can mean. Look there at the Grand Ole Opry. We will have that in my country some day."

As I listened, I realized how much we take for granted in this great country of ours. Men and women have died so we could be free to follow our dreams. Stanley helped to keep my dreams alive.

We met Pastor Oran Collins and his wife Mildred at the hotel. We followed the pastor to dinner and to his church, Harsh Chapel Baptist. While we were eating, I met Chris. In September of 1980, he was the only survivor of a car crash that killed three other teenagers. The young people had all been drinking before the accident. Chris had brain damage. He limped and stuttered tremendously. But he loved Jesus! He followed us to the service. Just before the service I also met Chad, a young man in a wheelchair. I began: "Someday, we won't need wheelchairs, crutches, and there won't be brain trauma. We will all have glorified bodies and be equal. Along with the rest of you folks, Chris, Chad, and I are going to walk on the streets of gold."

Day 90—Saturday, June 30

We were rowing by 8:15 AM. We were met by two police officers, Tom Cox and Rich Evans, in Gallatin. Their sergeant, Earl Hall, asked them to escort me all the way to Westmoreland, well past their jurisdiction. As we climbed the hills, they played music on his intercom. Just before we passed into Kentucky, I climbed a two-mile-long hill. It was hot and humid, but the officers cheered me on.

Just before lunch, the officers left. I glanced at my water bottle. It was empty! I tried to reach Jeff and Wanice on the radio. They were out of range. I went an hour without water. I was trying not to think about anything cold and wet, but to no avail. There were no stores nearby. Then a car pulled up. Three young people were inside. One of them asked, "Hey, how about a beer?"

I was worried about hurting my witness. I hadn't had a beer in a long, long time. I was so drained of fluids and almost out of my head with thirst, but I answered, "No, but thanks anyway."

The next three miles were tough without water, but somehow I made it through. I drank two quarts of water during lunch! But the lack of water had taken a toll on me. I had to stop for the day. My body informed me it had given me everything it could, and I listened.

We drove back to a motel, compliments of First Baptist, Donelson. We cleaned ourselves up, and then I spoke to Charlotte Road Baptist Church.

Jeff was leaving the following day, and I had four speaking engagements. I thought we had said good-bye for the final time in Phoenix. But Jeff and Judy were always open to do God's will. Despite his demanding job and bad back, he had come running when God said, "Take care of them."

Two weeks on the road together, along with the stress of the team change and doing the jobs of three people, had taken its toll on both of us.

We were absolutely exhausted! There was only one motel room left, so Jeff volunteered to sleep in the RV. What a friend!

Day 91—Sunday, July 1

We were at First Baptist, Donelson, at 7:15 AM. I spoke to both morning services to a total of about 1,000 people. Many visitors from the community and the Sunday School Board attended. After the second service, they presented me with a more than generous love offering.

Wanice took care of the logistics for the day and just let me concentrate on speaking. Jeff was dropped off at the airport and Don Bright was picked up. I was driven to Silver Springs Baptist Church to speak—then the pastor drove me to Riverside Baptist. Wanice and Don met me there. They walked in during the service. I introduced Don.

"Don has dropped everything to come to my aid. He is sixty-one years old and will be riding his bike the last 800 miles with me."

The church put us up at a hotel in Gallatin close to the start point. We were in bed at midnight. I had spoken four times on my day off!

Day 92—Monday, July 2

As Don put his bike together, I remarked that his nickname should be "Grizzly Adams." He wears a beard and is as tough as nails. Don had already biked through twenty-six states, even through Alaska and Canada. I was in good hands, and he could repair the RowCycle as well as anyone. In the near future, he would have to rebuild it completely. I was rowing and going by 8:30. But we could cover only twenty-five miles because of a speaking engagement four hours away. We finished outside of Glasgow, Kentucky, after climbing several hills.

We drove to Fort Campbell Army Base arriving at 3. I was met by DynCorp employee Jim Hayes and several media people. I was escorted by the police to the base gate, then by military police to the far side of the base. I rowed through the park and was met by a general who presented a plaque making me an honorary member of the 101st Airborne Division. (You can understand my "simpatico" with the 101st during the war in the Persian Gulf. The mayor of Clarksville, Tennessee, presented me the key to the city. I challenged the men and women to seek excellence in every phase of their careers and lives. I was also presented a check for paralysis research. Jim carried the boys on a tour of the base, and they saw several types of helicopters. We stayed on base that night.

Day 93—Tuesday, July 3

We drove back to Glasgow to the start point and were rowing by 10. The hills of Kentucky were like picture post cards and covered with farms. The old silos stood beside well-kept barns. Despite the panoramic view, I was so exhausted I stopped for the day in Camden after thirty miles by 3. We drove to Mammoth Cave National Park. I lay in the pool, too tired to move. Wanice did six loads of laundry and fixed supper. The boys played with sheep and chased ducks and geese. They had the best time they had experienced so far. Don was soon doing all Steve had done. I thought back to the two weeks when Jeff and I did everything by ourselves. What a miracle!

Day 94—Wednesday, July 4

It was a day off! We drove to Mammoth Cave National Park. There were seven different parts of the cave that could be explored. Despite my fatigue, I wanted to see the cave. I had gone to the largest cave in the world on the other side of the continent in Carlsbad. It seemed only right to see the longest cave in the world here. First, we went two miles around the perimeter of the park on Heritage Trail. At 2, Wanice and the boys went on the "Frozen Niagara" tour and I, on the tour for the disabled. I was accompanied by Mack, a fellow with cerebral palsy, and two rangers. My guide's name was Sammy. We were traveling at a snail's pace because of the speed at which most disabled people go, but I wanted to see as much of the cave as possible.

"Sammy, can we go ahead a little faster than the rest of the party?"
"Sure, let's go."

We took off at a brisk pace, and I kept up with him until we came to the end of the pavement. Soon we were on a hilly, rocky surface. I wanted to push the wheelchair myself, so we went ahead much slower. Soon the surface was craggy, and I slowed to a crawl, but I kept going. We eventually went as far as we could, and still came back to the elevator in time. Sammy declared that we had gone further than anyone ever had in a wheelchair. It was July Fourth, so we shot fireworks that night. Besides celebrating independence, we also celebrated having covered 2,750 miles. We had already broken the Guinness World Record for RowCycling *three times over.*

Day 95—Thursday, July 5

For having the day before off, I was extra tired! That should have been enough to tell me that something was wrong, but when I have a backache, I know what it is—a kidney infection! I took an antibiotic, but it was too late. My temperature started to climb. We started rowing at 8. I had no energy and was growing sicker by the minute. My legs spasmed as my spinal cord began to swell with the rising temperature. But I persisted in rowing. I was compelled not to stop.

We passed by Abe Lincoln's birthplace, Hodgenville. Don and I stopped for a few minutes and looked around quickly. Wanice took the boys for the long tour. I was becoming sicker! We went down a four-mile-long winding hill. Soon, we rowed by the "knob hills" Abe Lincoln had talked about. As we went over the hills I wondered if the Appalachians would be that steep. I hadn't seen anything yet!

We finally caught up with the RV at 12:30 after thirty-three torturous miles. I was too sick to eat. I began to sweat and shake. Within minutes I was shaking so badly with cold chills I was almost in convulsions. As my temperature rose, my legs began to have spasms (hypersensitivity) so severely I literally screamed in pain. Wanice covered me with a blanket as I shook with fever. I lay there for two hours in 100-degree heat and humidity, so cold I was under two blankets and still shaking. As the minutes passed, my condition worsened. Jason and Jonathan were sitting beside me as I sat up and, with a mean look, I stared at the next mountain. I knew that mountain stood between me and my dreams.

Jason was becoming very concerned for me.

"Dad, are you thinking that you can't make it because you're sick and the mountains are so big?"

"No, Son. I was thinking that there is no mountain too high or warrior big and mean enough to stop a person, if God gives him a dream!"

I set the blankets aside and crept back into the RowCycle. I began rowing again by 3. I had to go seven more miles to stay on schedule. I hit a three-mile hill. It was a small hill, but a mountain to me in my condition. I began fading in and out as my temperature rose! I began to cry with pain and was completely soaked with sweat. My mind was no longer rowing. It was back in time listening to my father . . .

"Boys, the Americans were trapped both by sea and land. A few more men arrived to help protect the fort, but they were badly outnumbered. The men knew that they could not win, but they fought anyway. They were prepared to die to keep the flag flying. The battle began. The British attacked the American forces just southeast of Fort McHenry. Next, the British attacked by sea. Fort McHenry was hit by 1,400 to 1,800 bombs from the British ships. Men were dying inside and outside as the attack continued. The Americans fired back yelling, 'We'll fight to our deaths to keep the flag flying.' "

"Keep the flag flying! Keep the flag flying,"was my battle cry as I fought the sickness and suffering. I was out of my mind with pain.

"What? What are you saying?" Don asked.

Realizing that I was talking out loud, my mind came back to the present as we began to go down a two-mile-long hill. I had gone forty-three miles for the day. I pulled into the parking lot, crawled into bed, and continued to shake. Jason came over to me and said, "Dad, I'll never quit again!"

"Son, I'll be proud of you no matter what. But the only way you'll feel good about yourself is to do your best. Whether you accomplish everything you try is not as important as giving it your best shot. If you try your hardest, you have nothing to be ashamed of."

If nothing else good happened on the trip, it had been worth it. I was teaching my sons that with faith in God and the proper attitude, anything is possible.

I shook all night with fever. I continued on the antibiotic. Everyone prayed for the infection to heal quickly. We drove to the famous "My Old Kentucky" Home State Park, built around the mansion made famous by Steven Foster. I was so weak, Don had to help me take a shower. No matter how old I get, when I'm really discouraged, I call my mom. Mom was a nurse and during the end of the conversation, she scolded me.

"Rob, I know you well enough to realize you won't stop. But don't take the antibiotic at full strength. Your heart rate is already high from the rowing. When you take an antibiotic your heart rate increases. Either stop and take the antibiotic, or continue and take it at half strength. It will take longer to heal, but at least you won't hurt your heart permanently."

I also called a friend, Julie Brantley, asking her to mobilize my friends in prayer. She encouraged me, even though she just had a baby and was herself in pain. Once again, I shook all night with fever and pains that wracked my body. It started raining again, and I prayed it would stop. If not, I would have to row, even with a fever, in the rain the next day. I finally fell asleep at 3 AM.

Day 96—Friday, July 6

We were met by the local media at 8 AM. I was very sick and tired, but I began rowing by 9:30 when the police escort arrived. We passed through Bardstown, went across a narrow bridge, and up a hill with no shoulder. I became awfully dizzy from the lack of food. Don stopped to talk with Wanice who was doing laundry. I took the wrong road due to my lack of concentration. I discovered my error, but I did not have a radio to give Don my position. I went back to the intersection and found the right road. I prayed that I would not get separated from Don in my weakened condition. I was out of water, and my temperature began to escalate again. After Don went ahead several miles, he came back the same way, hoping to run into me. We finally saw each other, and I some-how went another twenty miles before lunch. I stopped on every hill. I had no energy. I was expending too much energy on leg spasms and stomach cramps. I ate a small lunch and somehow went fifteen more miles. My fever began to break, and I sweated so copiously that I was totally soaked. I just wanted to quit and go home to my own bed. I was so grateful that Wanice was there to console me. I bathed and then slept all night for the first time in four days.

Day 97—Saturday, July 7

I woke semi-hungry for the first time in two days and ate a small meal. I was rowing by 8. We passed through Lawrenceburg. There was honey-suckle in the air, a slight tail wind, and birds serenaded us. The sun was out, and everything was green and lovely. I felt cheated that I had missed two days of my surroundings. I was totally overcome by the beauty of

Tennessee and Kentucky. Now that I was more aware of my environment, I noticed the local names. Within a few miles we passed Knister Knobs, Little Work Acres, and Lick Skillet. My legs continued to spasm so badly that it appeared I was having a seizure, and I grunted with every stroke, but the fever continued to drop. It was my third day of fever, and I was weak. I continued to sweat so much I drank a quart of water every half hour. Don told me about his adventures on bike trips he had taken, and it gave me courage. Don wanted to help me row, but he knew he couldn't. I had to do it all *myself*. The steep hills and winding roads had little or no shoulder.

We began descending a very steep one-a-and-a-half-mile hill. We took a sharp left turn at the bottom and ahead saw a quarter-mile-long bridge with no shoulder. I was already committed to cross and Don blocked the traffic for me. The other side was worse as we had to climb a mile and a half back up. Don continued to egg me on. I stopped several times per mile. I was not as dizzy, but I was pitifully weak. I had hardly any body fat left. I had lost five pounds in the last two days. We stopped in Versailles for a break. I needed to eat but couldn't. Then a man walked up.

"Hi, my name is Dennis. I own the Dairy Queen here. I heard about you guys. Let me get you some milkshakes for refreshment."

Although I could not eat, milkshakes sounded good. I drank three. Dennis was a Godsend. With my strength rejuvenated somewhat, we pressed on toward Lexington.

There were horse farms everywhere on the green rolling hills. We stopped at forty miles for a break and snacks under a huge oak tree. Don remarked that the tree was 100 feet high and 100 feet wide. As we began again we saw white fences that went in all directions and disappeared over the horizons. Everywhere we looked were miles of beautifully landscaped horse farms. We stopped on the corner of Highways 68 and 60 with forty-four miles behind us. We went to a hotel compliments of Gardenside Baptist Church. I ate my first real meal in three days— prime rib. I relaxed in the comfort of the hotel.

The fever had passed, but the next challenge was just around the corner. I had fourteen weeks and ten states behind me. However, I still had three weeks and three states to go. The finish would have to come from the heart because that was all I had left.

14

And Darkness Fell—
Never Doubt in Darkness What God Has Shown Us in the Light

Day 98—Sunday, July 8

Gardenside Baptist Church was troubled. They had nearly split. God gave me the words to build them up. I realized the difficulties I had suffered that week could have stopped me from speaking to three churches scheduled that one day. Channel 36, ABC, came to the church after the service. Next, we went to a picnic and spoke to Tates Brook Baptist Church. NBC came out and filmed for half an hour. Don drove us from the Lexington area to Bardstown Baptist Church. It was a lovely old church with a huge pipe organ over 100 years old. Ornate stained-glass windows adorned the walls and ceiling. The youth had just returned from camp, and revival had broken out. During the service, everyone knelt, prayed, and praised God together.

We drove back to Lexington thoroughly exhausted. If I had taken the day off like I probably should have, God could not have used me.

There was a mystery about my schedule that had remained up until that very moment. After announcing my desire to "Row Across America," my speaking schedule was filled within two weeks. As a matter of fact, I accepted 100 speaking engagements for the 120 days of the trip. I began turning down prospective engagements in all areas but one. The last week through West Virginia was totally unscheduled. It defied logic that not one group called me from that state. I was thinking about that when I felt I should look at a map. An alternate route practically jumped off the page. However, the route was about 100 miles further.

"But God, I'm just getting over being sick. I'm tired, and I could do with a week of no speaking."

"Rob, if I am for you, there is no power that can stand against you."
The Voice of the Holy Spirit was loving and kind, not demanding. He
was gentle yet commanded respect. That still small Voice had not mislead
me yet, so I listened. Instead of passing through West Virginia, we were
going all the way north to Columbus, Ohio, east through Pennsylvania,
and finally south to Baltimore and Washington D.C. I would have to
average forty-five-mile days with only one day off in the last two weeks.
Usually, after five straight days, I could not go on. Could it be done? Was I
going to believe in what I had been preaching or not? I discussed it with
the team, and we decided to follow the new route.

Day 99—Monday, July 9

I called about two scheduled radio station interviews and then met our
police escort in downtown Lexington at 8. It was two cars and a motorcycle. As a matter of fact, I had met the mother of motorcycle Officer
Garner in church the day before. Sergeant David Childer and Officer
Debra Plunkette were in the cars. They were incredibly efficient as escorts. The motorcycle went ahead to the next intersection while one car
was in front and the other in back.

"Why are you guys so good as escorts?" I asked during a break. Sergeant Childer answered proudly, "The last escort we gave was to the
Queen of England who was in the area buying horses."

We passed more large, well-groomed horse farms. The view was colorful—sculptured meadows and green pastures. The countryside was covered with roses, huge gates, and white fences that seemed to go into
infinity. Slowly the hills became larger and steeper, and we finally ran
into a three-mile-long hill.

I was instructed to pull over. Three deputy sheriffs swung in behind us
and replaced the Lexington police. Officers James Bartlett, Terry Pollitt,
and Stanley Buchanan continued the escort. I made fantastic time because I did not stop for breaks. They escorted us all the way to Nicholas
County. I stopped in complete collapse in front of a military academy. We
were met there by a rescue truck.

"Your request for an escort went all the way to the mayor. And I'm
him," said Frank Hughes with a smile. He explained that this was the
county's only vehicle. It was the one and only escort we received from a

mayor. The county was sparsely populated and strangely barren of buildings and civilization. Within the morning, we had gone from one of Kentucky's larger cities to one of its most unpopulated counties. Both had been beautiful in their own way. Mayor Hughes led us all the way across the county.

Reporters from three newspapers came out. We went thirty-three miles by lunch and Frank's wife, a nurse, stopped to take my life signs. Despite just getting over the fever and taking antibiotics, my blood pressure was 120 over 70, and my pulse was back down only two minutes after rowing.

"You're in incredible shape! Your temperature's normal," she brightly announced.

After four days, my infection was under control, and my strength was back. I believed that my healthiness was the result of obedience in going the extra miles through Pennsylvania. As I did constantly, I thanked my Lord and Savior.

After several more hills, we finished at forty-seven miles. We drove to Blue Lick State Park for the evening. The hills and thick woods covered the countryside and provided an incomparable backdrop as the sun set. As it did, I thought about the miles I had covered so far. I had crossed three time zones and was rowing in a fourth—almost 3,000 miles. What adventures lay ahead I was not sure, but I was confident that God had met all our needs and was capable of meeting those in the future.

The boys and I swam in a large pool. Wanice did five loads of laundry and cooked a huge meal. I ate four large plates of food. "Oh, no! Rob's appetite is back!" Wanice exclaimed in mock alarm, with a smile on her face, of course.

Day 100—Tuesday, July 10

You guessed it. I was rowing!!! We passed through Maysville on the Ohio River, surrounded by impressive hills. Don and I reached a speed of thirty-five on the hill and were met by the Maysville police at the Ohio River Bridge. We were in Ohio!

We took 41 north out of Aberdeen and slowly climbed the mountain on the other side. The heat bore down on us. Soon the road became narrow and crooked. After ascending another mile, we saw a heartbreaking sign: *Bridge Out—Road Closed.*

We had to go all the way back down the hill and start over at the bridge. We followed the river for ten miles and then began our trek over the hill again. We were met by the Maysville and Manchester press.

Bob, one of thereporters, had a disabled son. "You've inspired my son to keep fighting back against his disability. He's a real fighter, but he gets depressed and feels like there's no use."

"Tell your son that giving up hurts more than finishing. Temporary pain along the way is nothing like the long-lasting pain of quitting.

I gave him a book before beginning the climb again. I hurt badly, but I dedicated the ascent to Bob's son and kept going. We stopped at a fruit stand for a snack. The owner graciously gave us some fruit. Don and I gobbled it down. Don told her what we were doing and how sick I had been. She spoke with tenderness: "I hope this helps you. You've helped me to try harder." There were tears in her eyes as she handed me fruit and hugged me.

We passed through the hills of Bridgeport and went over forty miles. We turned right on 41 to West Union up a steep hill and were met by more press. We passed through Duncanville, and I was convinced more than ever that I must finish the "Row Across America" with my heart. My body had given all it could. I rowed another four miles. All my strength was gone as it began raining and hailing. That was the first hail we had encountered. The odometer read forty-seven miles for the day.

We decided to spend time at Bail Hollow Lake Park, situated by an immense lake comletely surrounded by verdant hills. Except for hard-working Wanice, I was helped by total strangers over the sandy beach to the lake. We swam in the lake until a fierce electrical storm chased us out. A lifeguard pulled my wheelchair through the sand in the rain. It was "Good night, sweetheart" at 9 PM.

Day 101—Wednesday, July 11

We were rowing by 8:15 AM. There was heavy fog all morning. After turning right onto Highway 41, we rounded the corner and beheld a mountain. The road was so steep it looked like a wall. The incline was two miles long, and my arms were in agony. That was nothing compared to what lay right ahead. We turned right onto Highway 32—then encountered a three-mile hill. After the first mile, the trucks were moving only fifteen miles an hour past us. The next two miles had to be conquered from the heart. Once again I was beyond pain to semi-consciousness. There were hundred-foot walls on one side of the road and a sheer cliff on the other. Up, up, up we went as though there were no end to it. We realized this was nothing compared to the Appalachians ahead. The top was green with rich pasture. It had been the toughest mountain since El Capitan.

Don and I proceeded to Waverly. We realized we had missed Wanice somewhere, and Don rode back ten miles to the intersection she had missed. I made phone calls while I waited for the RV to return. We stopped at 3 PM for the day with forty-five miles behind us. We drove three hours to Cincinnati and spoke to a local church which later put us up in a hotel.

I called Steve and gave him and Kristi tickets to fly to Washington, D.C. I learned that my entire family was going to be there.

Day 102—Thursday, July 12

Rain poured down (but, thank God, we didn't have a drought!) as we drove three hours back to Waverly. The landscape was shrouded in dense fog—visibility almost zero. Our still being alive after literally thousands of cars and trucks scarcely missed us and our going through Sahara-like heat and then the contrast of torrential rain, tornado and flood conditions, plus dense fog on the edge of mountain abysses, loose gravel, and falling rocks . . . was a miracle! No doubt about it, but we weren't there yet. We were in a dreadfully dangerous predicament. Next we ran into road construction that reduced four lanes to two.

"How long is this?" I asked a fellow in a truck.

"Over two miles, all uphill. What are you doing out here?"

I explained. He introduced himself as Glen Coleman. "I'll escort you with my vehicle," he offered.

"I don't want to slow down traffic or get you in trouble."

"Would you rather be dead?" Glen asked.

"No, that would mess up my day. Let's go."

He escorted Don and me all the way through the construction. He stopped Wanice and the boys. He even told our boys what a tremendous dad they have. (Honest, I didn't pay him to say that!)

We passed by Chillicothe with the north wind directly in our faces. Highway 23 turned into an interstate and we saw a sign: *No Bikes Allowed.* Sounded familiar. We were forced to pass through the center of town. Rain, rain, rain. The local press came out in the rain. Newspersons will work under the most adverse conditions. May God bless them for worthy efforts! Just then we barely heard Wanice (on the radio) as she passed on the interstate looking for us. We called her before she was out of range. She turned around and found us as we took side roads to Circleville. The press was there, too. Most of the media people asked very intelligent questions, but occasionally someone had a whopper.

One reporter turned to me and inquired, "Did you train for this?"

Don began to laugh. Realizing it was a rather unnecessary question, the reporter laughed, too.

Soon after, I passed a man in a wheelchair at a gas station. "I was hit by a car in 1973. I've never given up, but I've never attempted anything like you're doing. You've challenged me to push myself harder," he asserted. God knew I needed to hear comments like that, or maybe I would have given up. Praise Him for the encouragers! Determine that you will be one.

The terrain began to flatten out as we entered Northern Ohio. We passed through a heavy farming area with agricultural equipment everywhere. We went forty-six miles, still in the rain. "It rained all day the day I left . . ."

Day 103—Friday, July 13

Rain. Our crew was taking on the identity of rowing, riding frogs! We were at it by 8. Just before rowing into Columbus at 10, the rain stopped. We turned right onto Main Street. Tall buildings towered over us in heavy traffic. We received a motorcycle escort from Officer Tommy Williams. As I talked with him, he showed us the crime spots.

"See that man over there? He's selling drugs out of that briefcase. See that corner? Two murders occurred right over there." Those kinds of observations, unfortunately, can be made about most any city, town, or county in the nation. And it's because the message of God's Word is not going out enough and then not sinking in.

He continued to talk as we moved out of the city into the suburbs of East Columbus. Within an hour, we were back in the country. We stopped for lunch and Tommy ate with us. However, after moving so slowly with us, his motorcycle battery had gone dead.

Tommy turned to my two boys, "Guys, the police are here to help you, but every once in a while, you have to help us. How about pushing my motorcycle to start it?"

The boys lit up. They were actually going to help a huge six-foot-four-inch policeman. They did it. Of course, they bragged about it for days.

We traveled another fifteen miles through the country. We saw deer standing in the fields on the sides of the road. Tommy escorted us until our row for the day was over.

There was one dangerous feature about the RowCycle. The brakes were on the row arms, which was fine until going downhill. I would let go of the row arms and hold onto the side of the RowCycle frame in order to balance myself. This meant that I was without brakes. Don and I had talked about it, and he had bought the parts necessary to put the brakes on the side of the frame. It worked well. With the Appalachians all around, it was a vital alteration. It probably saved my life one week later. Oh, it rained all night again.

Day 104—Saturday, July 14

At 6:30 AM, I heard someone walking around outside the RV.

"Here it is. This RV says 'Rowing Across America.'"

There was a knock on the door. Don answered.

"Becky! Paul! I'm so glad you could come."

They were old friends of Don's who had driven two hours to see us off that morning. We talked for about an hour waiting for the rain to stop. It didn't, so I began rowing at 7:45 and let Don spend time with Becky and Paul.

The green, rolling hills and farmland eased my pain. Don caught up with me just as we were about to pass through the hills of Zanesville. I squinted at Don in my mirror. He looked unusual but I could not figure out why. Suddenly I noticed he was wearing moccasins. I asked him about it.

"Becky and Paul took Wanice shopping for food just as I was leaving. She locked the RV and left before I could get my shoes."

At 10 AM, a cable broke. Wanice was out of radio range. We needed the RV in order to replace the cable. We prayed and three minutes later, Wanice pulled up. Forty five minminutes later, we began again. Soon I was traveling over thirty down a long hill. The water was so deep my tires were throwing it high into the air. The front tire threw water and dirt right into my eyes, temporarily blinding me. I applied my brakes, but they were so wet and oil-slick they would not work. I was out of control! The slightest move, even wiping the dirt out of my eyes, would have made me crash. There was nothing I could do but ride it out. I continued to brake while trying to see. The water hit me in the face so hard it hurt. I barely saw a turn up ahead and leaned just in time. Finally the bottom of the hill was in sight. My fingers were white from squeezing on the brake handles. I finally started to slow down. Because of those conditions, I never knew how fast I had been going. It was probably close to forty MPH. I came to a stop. I had made it! I shouted, "Thank You, Lord!"

Don caught up with me.

"Why were you going so fast back there?"

"I couldn't see or stop!"

Don turned white with fright, and we paused for him to dry the brakes off. He told me of similar adventures in Alaska.

The week before, it had rained so hard that the sewers in Columbus had backed up! Now with another week of rain, floodwater was everywhere.

Going through Zanesville, we passed the stately city hall and met the press there. After beginning again, we confronted a big hill east of Zanesville. I had no strength left, and we called Wanice to pick us up. She did not answer, so we continued. The rain and hills blocked our radio signals. In an hour we went only a mile and a half. The road was very winding and steep. I hit another hill! Same conditions—flood stage and poor visibility. It took one hour to go one more mile. We finally caught up with Wanice at thirty-three miles by lunch. How was I going to finish the day, much less how I was going to go twelve straight days through the much bigger mountains to come? I need not repeat my litany of depleted energy and pain. After lunch, I took a one-hour nap. Don and I started again. We went another eight more miles uphill. We drove back to Columbus and hooked up to Mayes Road Baptist Church.

Day 105—Sunday, July 15

I spoke to the church and then met with the Columbus media folks in a church parking lot. We drove back to First Baptist Church of Waverly. It had rained so hard the water was rising fast. It reminded me of the Johnny Cash song, "Five Feet and Rising, Papa." Many area roads were being closed. Upon arriving, the pastor walked over to the RV. He was very disorientated and almost fell as he walked up the steps.

"Are you OK, Pastor?" I asked.

"Yes, I'm fine," he responded, quickly changing the subject. After a brief discussion, he led me to his study and closed the door.

"You asked me if I were all right. Well, I'm not. You see, I had stomach cancer. I had a reaction to chemotherapy and fell into a two-month coma. I have permanent brain damage! Speaking is very difficult, and preaching is next to impossible. The church has been very supportive and has stuck by me. But I think that we all need a word from God on permanent disabilities and our reaction to them."

"By the way," he said, "you received a package from Texas."

Six families from my church had sent us a Texas-sized basket of fruit. The card read: "We are praying for you; we know you can do it! We love you." Constant cheering up from home was a tremendous boost to me physically and mentally.

I spoke to the youth at 6 PM and pointed out the challenges of the trip. They sat in rapt attention. Next I preached to the entire church.

"If I did not believe in the next life, I would feel cheated. But I do believe in the life to come. This life is so short, do our little disabilities really matter in the broad scheme of things? I think we should just concentrate on the things we can do, and do them well. Don't worry about the things you can't do as well as others. God can use you right where you are, regardless of your shortcomings. Think about it. God used little David to slay Goliath. He did not choose a mighty warrior. Our abilities or disabilities are not nearly as important as our availability. When I look at you, I see a person. When God looks at you, He sees unending potential."

It was one of the last services until Washington. It was highly emotional. I could barely finish. The pastor closed the service and cried. He testified that I had emboldened him to "keep on keeping on."

We drove back to the starting point and slept in a gas-station parking lot.

Day 106—Monday, July 16

My hands hurt so badly, I could barely touch them. The skin was bleeding because of rowing in the rain. Rowing by 8. My back, stomach, arms, and hands demanded "Stop!" I actually talked to them, asking them to give me only two weeks more. I promised them: "Then I'll let you rest. OK?"

Just before we reached Cambridge, a young man passed us on his bike. He was shocked to see how hard I was working to move the RowCycle up the hills. He was a college student biking from Saint Louis to Baltimore.

"Hey, we're going through Baltimore, too. What route are you taking?" I asked.

"I'm going just north of Wheeling, West Virginia. I don't want to mess with the mountains there. Avoid Wheeling Hill if you can. It's a killer."

I didn't tell him that was the route we had chosen. His words rang in my ears. I wondered if they were prophetic? He rode with us for several miles. He simply could not believe how far I had come just using my upper body. He left us as we were entering Cambridge. There we met the media. I never wanted media exposure for Rob Bryant but for the Lord. God is first. Second, I wanted to raise funds for paralysis research.

While I was talking with a newspaper reporter, a man wearing tattered clothes walked up. He interrupted me and stuck out his hand to shake mine.

"Hi, my name is 'Crazy Bill.' I've never worked and I never will. I've traveled far, and I've traveled near. All that is important is my next beer." Give him credit for being a poet, anyhow.

I shook his hand and informed him I was raising money for paralysis research, not his next beer. I also suggested that he would not need a beer if he found a job and did something with his life. He stared at me blankly and then walked to the next person on the street. He started his routine again. "Hi, my name is 'Crazy Bill,' I've never worked . . ."

I thought back to the old man who had wished he could have done something when he was young. Now here was Bill, a relatively young man who was throwing away his life. One of them thought it was too late to do anything; the other had his whole life in front of him and was wasting it. I was not sure which one was worse.

We stopped at I-70 for lunch and napped a few minutes. We were on I-70 for eighteen miles. The interstate was a snap. I thought about what we said way back in California: "Interstates are for cars and wimps." Eventually I-70 merged back with Highway 40. I could not believe what I saw ahead. Highway 40 looked like another wall. It seemed to go straight up. I thought it was an optical illusion. When exiting I-70, we had to go down a hundred feet and circle around to the right. I found myself at the bottom of an incredibly steep hill. It varied from an 8 to 10-percent grade for the next two-and-a-half miles. This came at the end of the day, and I struggled along at one mile per hour for over two hours. One stroke at a time. One minute at a time. I thought of that Marijohn Wilkin song, "One Step at a Time." One row at a time, sweet Jesus. One row at a time. Only Jesus and His nature around me momentarily removed my mind from the excruciating pain. All along the route, my bloodshot eyes feasted on luscious green hilltop pastures with thousands of cattle. Like His Word declares, He owns rivers of oil and cattle on a lthousand hills!

We stopped at forty-nine miles on the outskirts of Wheeling, West Virginia. We drove to Bark Camp State Park. It was a deliberately planned primitive park—designed with a frontier, pioneer atmosphere. The air was cool as the boys played with other children in a large playground. The boys also explored the long trails. We ate a large meal outside on a picnic table and thanked God for the success thus far. Of course, we weren't aware of the surprise (not pleasant) that awaited us the following day.

Day 107—Tuesday, July 17

We ate breakfast on the picnic table and watched a new day dawn created by the Master Painter. We were rowing by 8:30 and were still climbing. We passed through Saint Clairsville and met the local media. Just then a rather thin man, clad in shorts, passed us. He stopped and marveled at the RowCycle.

"Hi, Mate. I'm an Englishman riding a bike from Washington, D.C., to LA."

"You're kidding! We're doing the same thing except heading in the opposite direction. We're almost there," I gushed as we shook hands. As soon as he touched my hand, I cringed in pain, but I was totally enthralled with his accent and what he was about to say!

"You mean you just use you upper body with that bike? You guys don't know what's up ahead on this road. I've ridden all through Europe, and I've never seen anything steeper."

I didn't want to hear any more bad news, so I changed the subject and filled him in on our trip thus far. We talked a few more minutes, then took each other's pictures and moved on. It was the second time in two days we had been warned about what was up ahead. I wondered if it was merely coincidence or a word from God. I was about to find out!

We were only five miles from Wheeling when we went down a four-mile-long hill. I reached a speed of thirty-five. In downtown Wheeling, Don and I crossed huge suspension bridges that were tremendous engineering achievements. The hills surrounding us in every direction appeared to be straight up and down. I was stopped twice by local media, and a network appearance was scheduled. One of the reporters warned us of "Wheeling Hill." It was a 10-to-12-percent grade up and the same going down. The trip up was tediously slow, and I broke a cable and spring due to the pressure on the row arms. The pressure per stroke was over 100 pounds. I pulled on the handles 1,200 times at that pressure up that one grade.

We finally went over the top and began our descent. I was moving over forty for the first time of the trip and finally slowed to thirty on a slight grade. We rounded the corner when I saw it coming. A manhole cover rose above the smooth road. I began braking and slowed to twenty-five when I hit it. I began careening wildly out of control. Everything seemed to slow down. My back wheels began to come up off of the pavement one at a time as the RowCycle crazily swerved out of control. Suddenly I flipped the RowCycle over. My head hit the pavement so hard it cracked my helmet almost in two. My ears began to ring, and my head began to pound as though I had been hit with a baseball bat. The RowCycle flipped once more, and I began sliding on my back. The road was ripping the skin right off my back, and there was nothing I could do about it. My right leg came out of the foot straps, swung wildly, and hit the pavement hard. Sparks flew as the metal on the side of the RowCycle scraped the road. Finally the RowCycle came to a stop as my shoulder hit the curb.

Two men named Tom and Gene jumped out of their car, and a policeman stopped to direct traffic. Don, Tom, and Gene reached me as I was trying to sit up, but my head was reeling, and I couldn't regain my balance even to sit up. I looked at the RowCycle. The frame was bent and cracked. Every chain and cable was broken and torn. The American flag on the back was on the ground. The sight of the flag and my pain caused me to travel back in time to another American flag.

"Boys, the battle continued for two days. The American losses were extremely low so the British increased their attack. The ships pulled closer and began blowing the fort apart. Men were dying and ships were sinking as the battle raged on through the night. The American land forces fought so hard and killed so many of the enemy that the British troops moved back.

"Meanwhile, a man named Francis Scott Key had been captured by the British. He watched the battle with horror from his ship. During the day, he knew that the Americans were still winning because he could see the huge American flag flying bravely over the fort. But during the night, the only time he could see the flag was when a bomb burst in the air near it. He watched helplessly as the British continued to dismantle the fort. Boys, listen to the words of the second verse of 'The Star-Spangled Banner.' It's more of a prayer than a declaration. It says that if men are fighting for what is right, then God surely has to help them. Suddenly, during the middle of the night, the battle was over. The British dispersed in every direction. But who had won? It was pitch black, and Key could not see the flag. The smoke from burning ships was so thick he could hardly breathe. He held his breathe waiting for the sun to rise. Whose flag was flying over Fort McHenry?"

I slid over to the flag and picked it up. "I'll keep it flying, Dad," I whispered.

I saw Wanice running to me. I had difficulty focusing my eyes and everything still seemed to be moving in slow motion. Don and Wanice put the RowCycle on the back of the RV, then lifted me into my wheelchair. Tom, Gene, and the policeman led us to the hospital. The doctor informed me that I had received a mild concussion, a broken toe, and a deep puncture on my right leg. I had scraped my arms and shoulders and had a large bruise on my right shoulder. It hurt so badly I could hardly raise my arms. But most painful was the ripped skin on both shoulder blades. I was raw and had several skin burns. The doctor told me that the burn on my foot from weeks ago was infected and also needed immediate attention. I realized that this damage to my body was going to cause agony on each stroke. The thought of moving my arms and ripping the skin on my back was almost more than I could bear.

Thank the Lord, we had planned on taking the next two days off. I was about to leave for Denver on the only planned excursion of the trip. This would give Don two days to rebuild the RowCycle and me two days to heal. I had a mammoth excuse for quitting. But the memory of the men at Fort McHenry spurred me on. I was going to finish or die! We drove to Indian Springs State Park. I lay in bed wondering where the strength for talking and autographing books the following two days in Denver was going to come from. I was going to meet Christian booksellers from all over the world.

Days 108 and 109—July 18 and 19

During the next two days, Don totally rebuilt the RowCycle. He replaced the tires, chains, cables, handles, and all other moving parts. I was thankful an expert like Don was along on the trip. God knew all along he was the man for the job. I was most thankful that he was obedient in coming. It made me think: *If we are not obedient to God, then He has to ask someone else to do our job who is probably not as well equipped.*

Don had had similar experiences on his trips and did not panic at all. Other than Steve, no one could encourage me through this like Don (Grizzly Adams) could. In the meantime, I flew to Denver and appeared for two days at the Christian Booksellers Association convention. I signed books on behalf of Broadman Press at a special booth.

I also talked with my employer. DynCorp was going to handle the Washington finish themselves! They were trying to secure the necessary permits and contact political leaders to meet me there in only eleven days.

We flew back to Wheeling and stayed in a church parking lot. We were all exhausted, and I would have no days off until arriving in Baltimore ten days later. The final challenge lay ahead. I was going to have to cross the Appalachians a tired, chewed-up man.

I had read books about decorated war heroes. They did not particularly think they had done anything brave at all. They were just too sick, tired, hurt, and hungry to care anymore. They came to the place where they didn't seem to care whether they lived or died. All they wanted to do was finish. They would pick up their rifle and charge into overwhelming odds—not because they were brave, but because they were too tired to care. The only way it would be over was to kill the enemy or be killed. Either way, it would be over. Those were exactly my feelings. My body hurt everywhere I could feel. My weight was way down; I had just recovered from the fever; and now there had been the wreck. As He had throughout, God would have to carry me—like the title of my first book, *Lord, Lift Me Up . . .* But either way, it would be over.

15

The Final Challenge—
Never Give Up on a Dream!

Day 110—Friday, July 20

An ABC television crew met us at the start point and asked me about my accident two days before. They had already talked with the hospital and knew my condition.

I said: "If God is for us, no power on earth can stop us!"

The RowCycle frame was bent, and we would not be able to repair it completely for the rest of the trip. I was rowing at an angle. However, Don had replaced and lubricated every moving part, so it actually handled better. My right shoulder was still very sore, but most painful were my ragged shoulder blades. On each stroke, I ripped the skin that was trying to heal. But after the first few hours I grew numb to the pain.

We turned north, left Wheeling, and headed toward Pittsburgh. I concentrated on the blue-green mountains all about us. I did not stop because I knew the numbness would leave, and I would have to row in pain again. We stopped at 12:30 for lunch. I removed the bandages from my back and took a nap. When I awoke and sat up, my back was hurting as though it were being slashed with a bullwhip. My shirt was stuck to the raw skin. Wanice soaked it in alcohol, then ripped it loose so I could row. I thought I would faint when the skin came loose. We replaced the bandages, and I was at it again. Praise God for the rain. It eased the hurt. As we were passing through Washington, Pennsylvania, the rain intensified. It poured down on the hamburger-like skin of my back. Water gushed out of manhole covers. Water rushed down the hills against us so hard it almost pushed me back downhill. I knew I would not quit and prayed I would not have to make further sacrifices on my health! Wanice escorted us through the city itself because of darkness.

We took Route 19 north to Pittsburgh in the afternoon rush-hour traffic. The rain continued, joined by fog. The last hill between me and Pittsburgh was three miles long and disappeared into a cloud. Because of the pain, I remember nothing of the hill other than the top. Wanice met us outside of Pittsburgh. Chalk up forty-two miles for the day. We drove through the tunnels near downtown. The boys are Pittsburgh Steelers fans and wanted to see Three Rivers Stadium. Downtown was interesting despite the rain and fog. Same scenario: it rained all night. My broken toe turned blue, and it seemed I hurt in every conceivable place.

Day 111—Saturday, July 21

It was still raining in the morning. I talked with the Pittsburgh police about my route. They said I had picked one of the most mountainous routes through the city but probably the safest. As we began, Wanice followed us through some construction before actually entering Pittsburgh. There were unbelievable grades everywhere. They looked absolutely vertical. We received twelve different police escorts through small cities south of Pittsburgh. Five or six radio stations broadcast our location, and people waved and honked at us. A television crew met us on Mansfield Bridge at the bottom of a hill. At the old West Fifth Avenue Bridge we were greeted by reporters. Police blockaded the traffic as I answered questions.

An hour later found us at the base of Crooked Run Road. The escorting policeman asked me to pull over.

"I can cut over three miles off your route if you want to go up Crooked Run Road. However, it is steeper than anything you've done today. Do you want to?"

I looked at my odometer to calculate the time we would save. *My total mileage was exactly 3,000.* I remembered all the days when I thought I could not go on. I had just taken one day at a time, one hill at a time, one stroke at a time, and here I was at 3,000 miles! Doxology!

All God wants us to do is to do the very best job we can do today and let tomorrow take care of itself, I thought. We stopped long enough to take a picture with four policemen. Encouraged by my odometer reading, I decided to take Crooked Run Road. The officer had not exaggerated. It was two miles long with grades from 10 to 12 percent. I was not sure what they were trying to tell me when I was followed by an emergency vehicle as well. Maybe they were expecting me to have a heart attack. I stopped for a break on a busy corner, already completely exhausted. The policeman jumped out of his car and directed traffic until I was ready to continue. We finally reached the top and stopped for lunch. Another Goliath had fallen!

"You know, the water sure tastes funny here," Don remarked at lunch.

We didn't think that much about it until later when Wanice filled up our water bottles. Don's was filled with mold. No wonder the water tasted so bad! We laughed about it for days.

It rained the rest of the day. We were going down a steep hill with no shoulder. We had passed police jurisdiction and were alone again. The visibility wasn't too good. Suddenly a small car appeared out of nowhere with a flashing siren and escorted us to the top of the next hill. The car motioned us over, and we met Neil and Joe, two volunteer fire fighters.

"There have been several bikers killed right here in these hills of Greensburg. You had better stop here for the day. We barely saw you out there! It's supposed to clear up tomorrow and will be safer."

I hated to, but we finished the day at thirty-eight miles. It had rained all but three days for the past two weeks. Surely it would stop soon.

Neil and Joe escorted us to their fire station, took Jason and Jonathan on a ride in a fire truck, and even gave them a fire helmet to keep. They led us to Fox Den Campground back in the mountains. It was surrounded by corn and oat fields and blue spruce trees. The office had hundreds of stuffed animals on the walls, and the gate was made of deer and moose horns. We ate, showered, and worked on the bike and RowCycle.

Day 112—Sunday, July 22

It was the first Sunday to row and the seventh consecutive rowing day. We read Scriptures for strength, and I had long talk with my body. "Just give me one more week," I reasoned with my aching muscles, cuts, and bruises. However, they were too numb and tired to care.

But—surprise!—God had scheduled a speaking engagement for us that night. We were rowing by 8:15 AM. We passed through Greensburg and saw a rough-looking hill ahead. What was that dark thing looming on the horizon behind it? As I came closer, I realized it was Laurel Hill Summit at Ligonier, the first of seven ridges of the Appalachians we had to cross. Passersby knew all too well what was ahead and cheered me on.

Wanice took Jason and Jonathan to see old Fort Ligonier. It was a good diversion for my family while Don and I pressed on toward our first ridge.

Don and I went by a church just letting out. They had heard of what I was doing, and those folks yelled, "God bless you!"

"You don't know what's up ahead," one person yelled as everyone applauded and prayed for us.

Jeff, a biker, passed us going to the top. He had always wanted to try climbing Laurel Hill Summit, and this was his day. He had trained for months to do it. With genuine empathy he looked at how hard I was working. Soon after, a man stopped and almost insisted that we put the RowCycle in his truck. I immediately thought of El Capitan where I had received the same sort of invitation. I didn't cheat there and was not about to cheat here. We started the climb from 800 feet at noon. The first two miles were a painful 8-percent grade. I proceeded at one mile per hour. Each time I would see a clearing, I would think, *Surely this is the top.* But it wasn't! After another hour, Jeff passed by on his way back down. He had made it. While he was talking to us, a truck stopped. We learned Jeff was a Sunday School teacher, and the truck was going to a gospel "singin'." We all paused and prayed.

After another hour of pain and determination, at 3 PM, I reached Laurel Hill Summit: altitude 2,694 feet.

I was out of breath and so tired I was almost incoherent when I met the Snellings. They were taking their daughter to a summer camp. Bill Snelling asked me several questions and seemed to have something in mind as he talked. I would find out shortly!

I also met a tough-looking motorcycle gang. I instinctively thought of avoiding them, but I felt I was supposed to talk with them. I was too tired to feel it if they beat me up, anyway, so I rowed over. Within seconds I was completely surrounded by the gang. The big, burly guys shook my hand, and the girls gave me a hug. I talked and witnessed to them. It was without a doubt the most unusual service I was a part of on the trip. I was thankful that my doubts had not stopped me. We were best friends within minutes. As a matter of fact, I would talk with them later by phone.

We had gone only twenty-nine miles for the day so I continued down a series of hills on the other side. The first one was practically straight down for two miles. We had descended over 1,600 feet, down to 1,000 elevation. I tried not to think about the fact that I was going to have to climb back almost to 3,000 feet six more times!

Bill Snelling met me at the bottom of the hill and had arranged for me to speak at "Summer's Best Two Weeks" youth camp. He escorted us to the camp which had vast acreage. We later learned the camp is widely recognized around the nation. People from all over send their kids there. It was beside a hidden lake, with waterslides and cabins tucked in the hills. Just before speaking to the assembly of kids in an ampitheatre, I talked to Jim Welch, the camp director. I asked him about a scar on his neck.

"Several years ago, I was passing an intersection when a man jumped in the car with me. Before I could say anything, he stabbed me in the back of the neck and left me for dead. I didn't know what had happened until the police found me wandering in the streets hours later. I owe my life to God and try to repay the favor by making a camp here for the kids to enjoy. You see, the kids are divided into two teams: the Romans and the Galatians. They compete fiercely, but the crux of the camp is Bible study. We lead more kids to Christ here than most large churches."

Day 113—Monday, July 23

It was the eighth row day. The grades averaged 9 to 10 percent everywhere. It was cool and foggy, but at least the rain had stopped. We challenged hill after hill. We calculated it to be up to 120 pounds per stroke at over 800 strokes per hour. As a matter of fact, Don had to walk beside me. He could not go as slow as I was going. At times we had only 300 feet visibility as we climbed tediously. I was robbed of the view on top of Allegheny Mountain, the second ridge. But I was secretly glad that I could not see the mountains ahead. We had gone only seventeen miles by lunch at Reels Corners. It rained off and on during the afternoon. I was afraid that I would not be able to make it, but somehow we had climbed back up to 2,904 feet. Don and I looked into the next valley and passed a sign which read: *9 Percent Grade, Next Six Miles.*

"That has got to be a misprint," I protested to Don.

We soon found that it wasn't. I was soon whizzing downhill at thirty-two miles an hour. "Whoopee," I hollered. It felt like a roller coaster, and I hardly cared if I "wiped out." We passed a large sign every mile which depicted the next mile of turns and switchbacks for the truckers. There was a truck pulloff ramp every mile. Wanice did not watch us. She was content to stay within radio range and pray. The rest of the afternoon passed, and we made a discovery. We were almost halfway through the Appalachians!

We celebrated that night at Shawnee State Park. I went with the boys for a long trek in my wheelchair. I was too tired and sore so the boys pushed me through the fabulous trails of the park. Upon returning, we talked with many of our neighboring RVs who had heard about us. They gave me words of encouragement and even brought wood for a fire. While we barbecued in the cool air, Wanice and I talked about a problem we had.

"Rob, how am I going to go all the way back to Pittsburgh to pick up Bob Peterson, yet stay with you through these treacherous mountains? I can't leave you without food, water, and an escort for six hours."

I didn't have an answer, so we prayed for God's wisdom on the subject. While I was showering and thinking of our dilemma, Jason ran into the shower.

"Dad, you'll never guess who's here. It's our cousin Cameron. He wants to know if he can ride the rest of the way to Washington with us."

We knew that Cameron was coming later in the week, but he was several days early. Later that night, Cameron told us he had been searching for us for days in the mountains. He was not sure why he had come early but felt he was supposed to be here. Cameron was not a professing Christian, but God used him anyway. Wanice and I knew why. God had just provided transportation for Bob from Pittsburgh to us.

Day 114—Tuesday, July 24

We prayed about where to meet Cameron and Bob that night; we decided we would wait until later in the day to see which city would be the closest. Cameron rode ahead twenty miles and dropped his car off before riding his bike back to meet us on the road. Cameron was an avid bike enthusiast and had won a few mountain bike races.

We passed through Bedford where my great-grandmother had been born and reared. I recognized many of the old buildings from my childhood. I wanted to see Grandma's house but didn't know the directions and who lived there now. I was really sorry I was going to miss her home. But we had a more pressing problem: Cameron did not have a radio with him, and we were directed to a different route than where Cameron was going to pass us. We were soon on the loop around Bedford. We sped to the other side to catch him before he entered Bedford. We accessed the road on the other side, when we almost missed Cameron coming the opposite way. He was going on the other side of the wide highway filled with traffic. I yelled at him, knowing that he would not be able to hear me. But he suddenly stopped and looked in my direction. He had heard me somehow. He joined us within minutes, and we moving once again.

The Lord was about to provide another miracle. Wanice had already done our wash and stopped at a store on the outskirts of Bedford. She was getting out of the RV when a lady stopped her.

"Are you related to Robby Bryant."

"My husband's name is Rob Bryant."

"Well, bless my soul! I am Betty Blevins, and this is my husband Lannie. We're second cousins of Rob's, and we live in his great-grandmother's house. You've got to come and stay with us tonight. I can't believe we ran into you here. We knew you were coming, but we didn't know when. We live on the other side of town, and we never shop here. But I saw an ad for something I really needed. Isn't God wonderful?"

Amen! I was thrilled almost breathless. God had just intervened again! We arranged to stay with them that night and received directions so Cameron would know where to return from the Pittsburgh Airport.

We climbed uphill to Breezewood where Cameron had parked his car. Then, I saw a sign that encouraged my tired body beyond words. There at the base of the next ridge, it read: *Washington, D.C.*, with an arrow pointing to the right. There were only two more mountains between me and my dreams. We ate lunch within sight of the sign, and I napped peacefully. Cameron and Jason left to pick up Bob. The mountain ahead was actually tougher than Laurel Hill. We snaked around for two miles to Breeze Hill Summit. We thought we were at the summit when we found we had to climb five more miles.

My body started yelling for me to stop. It tried to reason with me as if my brain were a separate entity. My body and brain talked with each other as my spirit stepped back to listen. My whole being hurt so fiercely that my body, soul, and spirit seemed to be three separate people. I just listened in as a fourth party as they talked, barely conscious of my surroundings. My body spoke first.

"Look, I said yes when you wanted me to continue through 1,200 miles of desert, over the Guadalupe Mountains against terrible head winds, through rain, heat, and cold. I said yes when you asked me to continue with little or no sleep, when you were stranded in Birmingham, even when you had a life-threatening kidney infection. I said yes when you wanted me to continue to row after the wipe-out and over the first five ridges of the Appalachians. Now it's your turn to say yes when I ask you to stop. I can't do this anymore. I'm drained. If I have to, I will shut down on you."

My brain was next: "I have always taken care of you. I have trained you well for this. Besides, I am only asking for another week of effort. I will give you the rest and attention you need when we are done, but right now I need your support. Rob just wants our help a little bit longer."

My spirit was not sure who was going to win the argument. My brain ignored the pain and was immmovable. Suddenly my spirit interrupted: "Didn't God deliver David from certain death when he faced Goliath?

Didn't God deliver Gideon from certain death as he faced tens of thousands of the enemy with only 300 men? Didn't God deliver Paul from certain death time after time on his missionary journeys? Surely God can get the three of us over this little-bitty mountain!"

I continued to row, waiting to see who was going to win the argument. I found myself sounding out words of praise. At first it was from my spirit alone. Soon my brain joined in, and finally my body shrugged its shoulders and agreed. We were together again as praises flowed.

"God created the beauty of this mountain. It is His footstool!"

Don joined in.

"God sent Jesus to the earth so we would know how to live."

"God spared my life in the fall and helped me to walk again. He can surely help me over this mountain."

"God helped me deal with Byron's death," Don said with a crack in his voice.

This continued all the way up the side of the mountain. We were near the top when Don began talking about his son's death. "One of the hardest parts of dealing with his death was that we never climbed Whitney together as we had planned. Soon after, Irene and I climbed Mount Whitney with a picture of Byron and dedicated the climb to him."

I was so caught up in what Don was saying that we were soon atop the mountain. I also dedicated the climb to the memory of Byron. Don and I cried as we descended the other side. We came away with new perspectives of ourselves and new truths, but we also left a part of ourselves behind. Don and I would never quite be the same after that day.

We had begun at 800 feet and climbed 2,195 feet to the top of Sideling Hill Summit. We would soon be back to 900 feet. We had climbed up and down several thousand feet on two ridges and nine separate hills.

After descending three miles, we began passing Amish farms. We passed a little Amish girl who was carrying freshly picked vegetables in her apron. She waved to us as we went by. We stopped and ate blueberries beside the road. We had gone thirty-four grueling miles. I could go no further. We drove back to Bedford to the Blevins's home.

I went to Grandma's grave. I knew she was not there but acted as though I were talking with her anyway. I don't believe we can communicatewith the dead, but I said, "Grandma, I've made it this far. I love you and miss you. I'll see you in heaven someday soon, and we'll share our adventures together."

Cameron finally arrived at 11 PM with my old friend Bob Peterson.

Bob was there when I prayed the first time after my near-fatal fall. He was there when I took my first step with braces. He was there when I crossed the finish line in Dallas after walking twenty-four miles in three days, a new world record for a paraplegic. It was only fitting he was here now.

Day 115—Wednesday, July 25

The boys remained behind with the Blevins's for three days. I said good-bye to them and told them a few of the adventures I had experienced in the old barn. I envied their simple lives. Their most challenging problem was who was going to play "North" and "South" in their next "play-like" Civil War battle.

We began rowing at Harrisonburg where we met a mean-looking ex-Marine who wore a Mohawk haircut. I remembered my meeting with the motorcycle gang and began talking with him despite his intimidating appearance. He turned out to be a truly nice guy who had suffered some personal pain that caused him to rebel against society. We gave him a book and pressed on. We went up the first part of the ridge and then proceeded up a two-and-a-half-mile steep grade. We sailed down a another steep grade into McConnellsburg. We were looking at the last of the seven ridges. The last! Not thinking about what it represented, we took the loop around the town and began our slow ascent. I was in my bottom gear and moving at one mile per hour. We climbed up for over five miles to the top of Tuscarora Mountain. Our average speed until lunch was only 2.9 MPH. Our average for the day was only 3.4 MPH. It was the slowest speed of the entire trip.

We had covered only fourteen miles by lunch at 2:30. However, we were through the Appalachians! We went another fourteen miles over small hills around Chambersburg. Now, my body laughed at them.

During the day, Bob had washed and cleaned the RV for Wanice. Six weeks on the road had taken its toll on Wanice (Superwoman) also. She was thankful Bob had come to help her. We drove to Caledonia State Park at the base of South Mountain. Honest, I ate five plates of spaghetti outside on a picnic table. We watched the squirrels play until dusk when fireflies filled the air. We laughed for hours as we all felt the tension lift from us. We had met the final challenge and won! Wanice celebrated the fact that there were no kids for her to be responsible for. She could really relax and enjoy the moment with me. Wanice and I talked about the accomplishments behind us. She held my sore hands as the sun went down over South Mountain.

16

A "Capitol" Finish—
Finishing What We Start
Is Worth the Pain!

Day 116—Thursday, July 26

Don (Grizzly Adams) had been picking on Cameron because of his strange eating habits. Don would eat anything that didn't move. He might even eat moving things that didn't bite back!

"I'm not picky. I just like things cooked a certain way. Of course, I don't like many of the vegetables, and I don't eat much red meat, and I don't like fried foods or foods made with milk. But other than that, I'm not a picky eater," Cameron noted as he poured apple juice onto his cereal.

We all burst into laughter as Cameron looked as us in wonder.

It was the first day since Ohio that Don did not have to walk beside me. We rowed up South Mountain, the last mountain on the trip. It was not nearly as steep or large as the Appalachians. As we descended a long, gentle four-mile grade, we had a panoramic view of green farmland ahead. Cameron left us to pick up his uncle, General Cecil Jenkins. Cameron had been a tremendous help. I hoped the relationship had been mutual.

We arrived in Gettysburg and went to the Eternal Peace Light Memorial at the Civil War Memorial. As we rowed past the various battle memorials, we shuddered at the thought of all the American lives lost there. The South had won every major battle until Gettysburg. The North's leadership decided that in order to win the war, they would have to win this battle. For that to happen, severe sacrifices would have to be made.

Likewise, the South, with inferior equipment, had made dreadful sacrifices. I equated them with the sacrifices my many friends had made to win this "Row Across America." It was nearly over.

Wanice and the boys, Steve, Kristi, Jeff, Don, Dad, Jane, Gary, Gerald, Bob,and David Allen all had sacrificed. We ate lunch there in the battlefields and thought about the 3,200 miles behind us.

We crossed over several more small hills and were in Maryland. We stopped at forty-seven miles and had a meal with my Aunt Ginny and Uncle Gunther in Westminster, Maryland. We spent the night with my cousin Martin and his wife. They lived in the oldest house in the county. Built in 1765, it was surrounded by history. The two-story home had a narrow pair of old stairs that separated the open one room below and the sleeping quarters above. The house was filled with antiques. It was as if we had stepped back in time over 200 years.

I went outside after supper. The stars were unusually bright. The moon hung over the hills to the west. I thought of the miles of pain and then looked east to the finish. "Finishing what we start is worth the pain," my body admitted to my mind and spirit. They both agreed and thanked my body for never giving up! We were asleep by midnight. Steve had flown in and would join us for the last two days of the trip. I was glad he was going to ride in with us because of the sacrifices he and Kristi had made.

Day 117—Friday, July 27

We were rowing by 7:45 AM, taking 140 South toward Baltimore. We could smell the ocean for the first time as we crossed the little hills. It was our eighth rowing day—and it felt like it. We were about to leave the lush, green hills for the last time. We were heading for two of the most prominent cities in America—Baltimore and Washington. The roads became busier and busier. Area television and newspaper people came out to interview us. We stopped in Garrison at thirty miles for the day. We drove to Reston, Virginia, for a scheduled speaking engagement at Dyn-Corp's corporate headquarters.

We were met by an escort of four motorcycle policemen. Jeff Wilson, Cameron, and my Uncle, General Cecil Jenkins, were there. The last time I had seen Cecil was in New Mexico.

We rowed onto the property to an incredible reception. Ahead was a phalanx of people. Hundreds were applauding and cheering. As I came to a stop, music began to play, and the crowd applauded for three minutes. I met Dan Bannister, president of DynCorp, as a band struck up "The Star-Spangled Banner." My emotions were getting the best of me as Mr. Bannister introduced several visiting dignitaries. He also had a surprise waiting for me.

"Rob, your efforts to raise money for paralysis research have not gone unnoticed by the employees of DynCorp. I would like to present to you this check on DynCorp's behalf. I also have another surprise for you. We know that this victory would not be complete without your father and stepmother being here. Lee, come on out!"

My Dad and Jane came running out of the building, and I hugged Jane and shook Dad's hand. I told the group the Fort McHenry story and closed with this statement.

"There is no mountain too high, no ocean too wide, and no warrior big and mean enough to stop us, if God gives us a dream."

I pumped hands and autographed books before rushing to Norwood Baptist Church with an entourage of cars following us. Wanice and I laughed, "There are more of us than the congregation."

We celebrated with Wanice, Dad, Jane, Cecil, Cameron, Don, and with Gary and Nancy Reisor. All were there but Steve.

Day 118—Saturday, July 28

I slept in the van going back through D.C. and Baltimore to the starting point. When we reached it, Steve was nowhere to be found! I thought we had missed him. Wanice called him at Grandma's house and woke him up. He told her that he was not coming! Although I suspected the reason, I would not find out why for two days.

Starting at 9, by 11 we were one mile into Baltimore County when the first police escort showed up. Before the end of the day, we were afforded seven different escorts. We were supposed to arrive at 3, but we made it by noon. I asked our police escort, Officer A. J. Hatcher, to escort us toward Washington for the sake of time. We planned on going as far as we could before jumping into the RV and coming back to the Glen Burnie Mall at the appointed time to meet with our family and the press. We were off again. We soon found ourselves on a shortcut that Officer Hatcher knew—Nursery Road. I was practically raised on Nursery Road, and we passed my Granny's house. We hugged and Granny cried.

Then, with city permission, we took Business 3 South. I heard the captain on the radio shout, "Go for it!" We soon traded police escorts for the final time on Highway 3. We moved along at over ten miles per hour as my adrenalin powered my arms to go faster than I had ever gone on flat ground. My heart was pumping out raw energy for my pulsating muscles. It was poetry in motion. My body was excited about the prospect of the trip being over. We finally stopped for the day. We had only twenty more miles to the Capitol on Monday.

But we had a problem. Time had fled from us, and we had only twenty-five minutes to go twenty miles through rush-hour traffic in Baltimore! It couldn't be done. The senior officer called the captain with a request.

"Captain, can I escort the Bryant's RV back to Glen Burnie Mall a little faster than they can go? I'm afraid that they will never make it on their own."

"No, they *are* on their own. We gave them an escort while rowing. I cannot give clearance for a high-speed escort during rush-hour traffic."

The officer looked disappointed. It was "totally awesome," to borrow from the Valley Girls, but we would actually make it. Wanice drove, and I cannot possibly explain the change in her personality. There was fire in her eyes as she sped like a whirlwind through the heavy traffic. She had become a NASCAR driver right in the middle of the nation's capital. She had turned into the feminine counterpart of Richard Petty, Darrell Waltrip, and Ricky Rudd, racing through the crowded streets, missing cars by inches. The rest of us watched in total terror as this possessed person, whom I had never known before, smiled at danger and laughed at possible death. We arrived within two miles of Glen Burnie Mall in the nick of time. Frankly, I was shaking as if I had Saint Vitus's Dance. Officer Hatcher met us there and escorted us to the mall. Two other policemen appeared out of nowhere to assist us across Ritchie Highway. We miraculously arrived at 3:05 PM.

My entire family was there including Jason and Jonathan, all three brothers, two sisters, two sets of parents, and grandparents. Our entire families had never been together before. There were also aunts, uncles, cousins, and old friends composing another 100 people. My family had worked awfully hard on media coverage. ABC, NBC, *The Baltimore Sun,* and other media were waiting for us there.

We went to Grandma's for supper where I talked with Steve about not riding into Washington with me.

"You didn't permit me to return after I told you there was nothing wrong with Kristi. You had no right to make that decision for me. You made Birmingham my finish line! I would feel like a liar riding in with you as if I had been on the whole trip." I let him vent his frustrations on me. I didn't defend my actions in any way, shape, form, or fashion. After all, I understood his fierce desire to finish. We had the same blood running in our veins. I was disappointed he was not riding in with me, but I understood.

We went to Granny's for a second supper as only Granny could cook. My older brother Mike asked if he could help me finish the "Row Across America" on Monday. Since Steve was not riding in with me, I was relieved that one of my other brothers was coming. Mike would prove to be a big help.

Day 119—Sunday, July 29

I spoke to Pennsylvania Avenue Baptist Church in Washington that morning. Mom's side of the family was there, along with Jeff, Don, Bob and Gary who had come to my rescue. Just before I spoke, the choir sang "Climb Every Mountain." Considering that I had just crossed every mountain range between the Pacific and Atlantic Oceans, the choice of songs was on target and also emotion stirring, to say the least. I was controlling my feelings until I made the mistake of looking over at Charles Worthy, the pastor. There was a tear running down his cheek. I lost it! After the service he explained, "Rob, I was just thinking about how agonizing that trip must have been." I scarcely brought my emotions under control before giving my testimony. One piece of human interest I had talked about across the nation was about my Grandmother's prayers.

"One reason I am 'walking'—even though it is walking by propelling myself with my upper body—is that my parents and grandparents had been praying. When a grandmother prays, the heavens open up, and

God's hand often moves. God does not even trust that to angels. I guess that God figures He might as well go ahead and do it, because grandma is not going to quit praying until He does."

We drove to the other side of Washington to South Run Baptist Church. Just before speaking, up pulled Murt. He was a quadriplegic driving a pick-up. He had made amazing strides in his physical therapy. He was moving his arms enough to drive and even play some sports. His pick-up had a crane for his wheelchair. I had sold my car in order to buy the RV. So I was without a car. I planned to buy one exactly like it when I returned home.

I spoke in an amphitheatre in the park. It was beside a lake, under the stars with the moon reflecting on the water. I closed by saying:

"Don't ever give up on your aspirations. If you are sure that God has given you a dream, don't let the enemy rob you of it. Besides, when you quit, you are saying that God is not big enough to accomplish what He has asked you to do. If we quit we are teaching our children by example to give up. As a parent, you might be the only glimpse of Jesus your kids see all day. Let your dreams be as big as God is."

After the service, I called Grandma to see if Steve had changed his mind. He had not. While talking with her, she told me, "Rob, that was the second most meaningful service in my life. The only service that was more meaningful was the one where I was saved as a little girl."

It was the last night of the "Row Across America." I gave the results to God. I had done everything I could do. Had DynCorp been able to get anyone to meet me? What was going to happen tomorrow?

Day 120—Monday, July 30

We received word there was not going to be a police escort! Too much was going on in the area, and they needed more advance notice.

We were rowing on Highway 140 by 8 AM. By 10 we were approaching Washington. Our entourage of cars and the RV consisted of Wanice and the boys, my uncle the General, and my brother Mike and his wife Shirley. The biking team consisted of Don, Cameron, my sister Kay, Brian who rode into Fort Worth with me, and two other friends from our church in Texas. We stopped long enough to pray for our safety. I asked Don to bring up the rear to watch the less-experienced riders. We finally arrived at Seventeenth Avenue where I was to take a left and go to the Capitol. I had just enough time to make it.

We started down Seventeenth Avenue. It looked awfully slummy to be the right area. We asked a policeman how to reach the Capitol. He informed us we were on the wrong Seventeenth Avenue.

"There are four Seventeenth Avenues. You are on Northeast Seventeenth. You need to be on Northwest Seventeenth. You are over thirty-four blocks away from the right road!"

I looked at my watch. It was 11:15. We had to go from Northeast Seventeenth Avenue to First Avenue, then back Northwest Seventeenth Avenue in forty-five minutes. It was almost the lunch rush hour, traffic was bumper to bumper, and we did not have a police escort. We hit construction at 11:35. Mike began blocking traffic for us, but we still had to stop at every light. We prayed for a police escort, and one showed up for a few minutes long enough for us to weave through the rest of the construction without stopping. We took a left on Northwest Seventeenth Avenue and passed the White House. Incredibly, we hit more construction. It was 11:45. We were directed to the west. My biking partners began stopping traffic for me, using their bodies as a shield. Mike continued to block traffic.

We arrived in the mall area. I could not believe it! We were on the wrong side of the Lincoln Memorial. It was 11:50, and we had almost two miles to go through dense crowds of people. Jeff was stationed at the Capitol with a radio and contacted us for the first time.

"We're waiting for you in the grassy area behind the Capitol. There is quite a group waiting for you here. You need to take the ramp around to the back of the Capitol. Where are you?"

Don answered, "We're over a mile away from you, stuck in the crowd. We're coming as fast as possible."

As the team continued to block the way for me, the memories of the trip began coming back to me! I thought about the mountains in the first three states, 1,200 miles of desert, El Capitan, 972 miles of Texas, the rain, hail, cold, and wind, the fever in Kentucky, the wreck in Wheeling, and finally the Appalachians. I was so thankful that no matter what hell had thrown at me, I had depended on God and kept going.

A few people stopped me, asking if I were the one "Rowing Across

America." I did not have time to pause, and the bikers helped me through the crowd. I hit gravel four blocks from the Capitol. I pulled on the handles as hard as I could, and the inches passed by. I arrived at the front of the Capitol at 11:57. We passed several congressmen walking by, and they applauded as I climbed up the ramp around the building. On turning the corner, there was Dad holding a sign of congratulations. As I looked at Dad, the final part of the Fort McHenry story came back to me.

"The battle was over. It was dark, and Francis Scott Key aboard his ship did not know who had won. He waited the long hours until the fingers of the sun began rising up on the horizon of the sky. Slowly he could see the outline of the fort and then the flag. But it was so dark the flag was colorless. Slowly as the morning sun rose higher, he could see it. The American flag was flying! The small American force had held off the attack of the much more powerful British Army. Boys, when you face challenges in your life, I want you to remember these men. They died for your freedom so that you could follow your dreams. When you quit, you make a mockery of their death. You are Americans. You don't have to quit in the face of adversity. Give it all you have, Boys! That's all they did, and that's all that you can ever ask of yourselves!"

As I passed Dad, I thanked him again.

I rowed under a large sign held by Mike and Shirley. Finally, I looked ahead and saw the finish-line tape held by our two boys.

Back in Kentucky I had told them, "There is no mountain too high, no ocean too wide, and no warrior strong enough to stop us if God gives us a dream."

We gave one another other a knowing look. They had been there. They knew what I had been through.

I passed through the tape. It was over. I had made it! I moved to the grassy area. My entire family was there. I was congratulated by a United States senator and several congressmen. I gave God all the glory and shared a few details of the trip with the press. I thanked my family individually by name and told how far each of them had come with me. It was over!

The "Row Across America" was honored with two entries in the Congressional Record, and two days later, the flag flown over the Capitol was in honor of my employer and me. I was presented a certificate of recognition signed by Arnold Schwarzenegger, chairman of the President's Council on Physical Fitness. I had raised tens of thousands for paralysis research. In addition, we received a letter from President and Mrs. Bush congratulating us.

We stayed in the Washington area for several days. But I had one last stop to make: Fort McHenry. I stood on top of the fort, with the flag flying proudly behind me. I told our boys the same story Dad had told me.

The RowCycle will soon be on display in the Smithsonian Institute. The "Row Across America" has been submitted to the *Guinness Book of World Records*. Steve and Kristi's baby, Katheryn Marie, was born on November 26, 1990. She is today a happy and healthy baby.

Once, a youth named David dared to walk into a field and face a giant with nothing but a rock and a slingshot. David won the battle because God gave him the dream. We all have Goliaths in our lives. It may be a sin that has you whipped, or a goal God has given you to do. Your Goliath is standing there bellowing at you. He is yelling that you are not big enough—your God is not big enough to slay him. But the smallest child can slay the greatest giant, if God gives him the dream. God—through you—can slay Goliath. Don't ever give up on your dreams!